THE STAG HUNT
AND THE EVOLUTION OF SOCIAL STRUCTURE

Brian Skyrms, author of the successful *Evolution of the Social Contract* (which won the prestigious Lakatos Award), has written a sequel. The new book is a study of ideas of cooperation and collective action. The point of departure is a prototypical story found in Rousseau's *Discourse on Inequality*. Rousseau contrasts hunting hare, where the risk of noncooperation is small but the reward is equally small, with hunting the stag, where maximum cooperation is required but the reward is much greater. Rational agents are pulled in one direction by considerations of risk and in another by considerations of mutual benefit.

The possibility of a successful solution depends on the coevolution of cooperation and social structure. Brian Skyrms focuses on three factors that affect the emergence of such structure and the facilitation of collective action: location (interactions with neighbors), signals (transmission of information), and association (the formation of social networks).

Written with all Skyrms's characteristic clarity and verve, his intriguing book will be eagerly sought out by students and professionals in philosophy, political science, economics, sociology, and evolutionary biology.

Brian Skyrms is UCI Distinguished Professor of Social Sciences, Professor of Logic and Philosophy of Science, and Professor of Economics at the University of California, Irvine.

To Adolf with all my best Brian

The Stag Hunt and the Evolution of Social Structure

BRIAN SKYRMS

University of California
Irvine

CAMBRIDGE
UNIVERSITY PRESS

PUBLISHED BY THE PRESS SYNDICATE OF THE UNIVERSITY OF CAMBRIDGE
The Pitt Building, Trumpington Street, Cambridge, United Kingdom

CAMBRIDGE UNIVERSITY PRESS
The Edinburgh Building, Cambridge CB2 2RU, UK
40 West 20th Street, New York, NY 10011-4211, USA
477 Williamstown Road, Port Melbourne, VIC 3207, Australia
Ruiz de Alarcón 13, 28014 Madrid, Spain
Dock House, The Waterfront, Cape Town 8001, South Africa

http://www.cambridge.org

First published 2004

Printed in the United States of America

Typeface Meridien 10/13 pt.   *System* LaTeX 2_ε [TB]

A catalog record for this book is available from the British Library.

Library of Congress Cataloging in Publication Data
Skyrms, Brian.
The stag hunt and the evolution of social structure / Brian Skyrms.
p. cm.
Includes bibliographical references and index.
ISBN 0-521-82651-9 – ISBN 0-521-53392-9 (pbk.)
1. Social structure. 2. Social action. 3. Collective behavior.
4. Social evolution. 5. Social networks. 6. Cooperation. I. Title.
HM706.S54   2004
301–dc21   2003051530

ISBN 0 521 82651 9 hardback
ISBN 0 521 53392 9 paperback

For Pauline, Michael, and Gabriel

It is true that certain living creatures, as bees and ants, live sociably one with another . . . and therefore some man may perhaps desire to know why mankind cannot do the same.

– Thomas Hobbes, *Leviathan*

CONTENTS

PREFACE

HOBBES picks up an ancient thread: "It is true that certain living creatures such as bees and ants, live sociably with one another (... by Aristotle numbered amongst political creatures), ... and therefore some man may perhaps desire to know why mankind may not do the same."[1] In our own time the question arises in greater variety and detail.[2] The problem of the social contract has been solved in many different ways at all levels of biological organization. To the ants and the bees we can add social amoebas, such as the cellular slime molds, and even social bacteria like the "wolf-pack" *Myxococcus xanthus*. Inside a human body, there is the society of organs – well known to the Greeks – composed of societies of tissues, which are in turn composed of societies of cells. The social contract for the body of a multicellular organism is written again and again in chromosomes in each cell. Chromosomes are societies of genes. Each cell also has a subsidiary contract with its mitochondria, formalized in their DNA as well as its own. It is evident that rational choice is not necessary for solving the problem of the social contract.

Hobbes thought that rationality was part of the problem. Ants and bees act together by instinct, not reason: "The agreement of these creatures is natural; but that of men is by covenant only, which is artificial."[3] Humans are tempted to defect

xi

by rational self-interest. After Darwin, the considerations that Hobbes raises appear in a different light. If an individual may profit by defecting from a covenant, then in evolutionary time a defecting mutant type might arise and undermine the social contract. The appeal to instinct ultimately leaves open the same questions. The fundamental problems of the institution of the commonwealth and of its stability are as much problems for evolutionary theory as they are for political theory. We are led from Hobbes's point of view back to that of Aristotle – man is a part of nature, and the state is not artificial but a creation of nature.

We may also follow Aristotle in a different way: "As in all other departments of science, so in politics, the compound should always be resolved into the simple elements or least parts of the whole."[4] But in resolving the complex into the simple we will follow Hobbes – for Hobbes was really the grandfather of game theory – in focusing on simple social interactions modeled as games. In analyzing these interactions, we will use Darwinian adaptive dynamics of evolution and of learning.

If one simple game is to be chosen as an exemplar of the central problem of the social contract, what should it be? Many modern thinkers have focused on the prisoner's dilemma, but I believe that this emphasis is misplaced. The most appropriate choice is not the prisoner's dilemma, but rather the stag hunt – thus the title of this book. The case for the stag hunt is made in the first chapter, and developed throughout. In the course of discussion, a number of other games receive attention, most notably a bargaining game, which deals with how the gains from collective action are to be divided, and a division-of-labor game, which implements a more sophisticated version of cooperation.

The key to the evolution of cooperation, collective action, and social structure is correlation. Correlation of interactions allows the evolution of cooperative social structure that would otherwise be impossible. Social institutions enable, and to a large part consist of, correlated interactions. How do interactions become correlated, and what is the effect of these correlations on the evolution of cooperative behavior? This book is an introduction to some ways of investigating these questions about the coevolution of correlation and strategy. Part I discusses the effect of interactions with neighbors. Part II considers the exchange of signals prior to an interaction. Part III embeds interactions in an evolving social network. Each part isolates a simple empirically motivated modification of the most thoroughly studied evolutionary model and shows how the modification makes a dramatic difference in the evolutionary dynamics of the stag hunt and related interactions.

The fundamental techniques and principles surveyed may plausibly be applied to other species as well as man, and at various levels of biological organization. The considerations of location, signaling, and network formation, introduced here in their simplest forms, are capable of being combined to form models of complex phenomena. For example, signaling might be combined with association. Cooperative types might use signals to find each other, associate, and help one another. This seemingly complex strategy is already implemented at the level of social amoeba, where in the slime mold *Dictyostelium*, a single gene codes for a protein that migrates to the surface of the cell and causes those having it to literally "stick together" in the formation of a multicellular fruiting body.[5] Although the topic of prime interest to us may be the formation of human social contracts by means of learning and cultural evolution, we should never lose sight of the range of collective action exhibited across the spectrum of living organisms.

As the development progresses, the importance of understanding the processes involved will become apparent. Observations that seem to be in equilibrium may not really come from a true equilibrium; true equilibria may never be observed.

Transient phenomena may be crucial to an understanding of real behavior. The dynamics of evolution and learning has to be taken seriously.

I have tried to present the essentials of the important effects of location, signals, and association and their impact on the evolution of the social contract in the simplest possible way. Technical analyses have been reserved for journal articles. Everything should be accessible to the reader interested in pursuing a naturalistic theory of the evolution of social structure.

ACKNOWLEDGMENTS

THIS book owes its greatest debt to two of my co-workers. Chapter 2 rests heavily on the research of Jason McKenzie Alexander, and Chapters 6 and 7 rely at critical points on the contributions of Robin Pemantle. Fuller references are given in these chapters. I owe most of my education in Hume's game-theoretic ideas to Peter Vanderschraaf. Ted Bergstrom improved my understanding of Maynard-Smith's haystack model. Jerry Busemeyer shared psychological data on reinforcement learning. Duncan Luce read the entire manuscript and made many valuable suggestions. An anonymous referee suggested the inclusion of a discussion of the three-in-a-boat: two can row problem. Persi Diaconis encouraged the investigation of association pursued in Part III and brought me together with Robin Pemantle. Many of the ideas in this book were first tried out in a seminar on evolutionary and quasi-evolutionary models that I coteach with Louis Narens and Don Saari. The exposition owes much to feedback from that seminar and also from an undergraduate course in philosophy of biology that I coteach with Francisco Ayala and Kyle Stanford. The University of California, Irvine, provided computer time for some of the larger simulations. Other simulations by Bill Harms, Doug Hill, Jason McKenzie Alexander, and Peter Vanderschraaf have also informed the present discussion.

1

THE STAG HUNT

THE STAG HUNT

THE Stag Hunt is a story that became a game. The game is a prototype of the social contract. The story is briefly told by Rousseau, in *A Discourse on Inequality*: "If it was a matter of hunting a deer, everyone well realized that he must remain faithful to his post; but if a hare happened to pass within reach of one of them, we cannot doubt that he would have gone off in pursuit of it without scruple."[1] Rousseau's story of the hunt leaves many questions open. What are the values of a hare and of an individual's share of the deer, given a successful hunt? What is the probability that the hunt will be successful if all participants remain faithful to the hunt? Might two deer hunters decide to chase the hare?

Let us suppose that the hunters each have just the choice of hunting hare or hunting deer. The chances of getting a hare are independent of what others do. There is no chance of bagging a deer by oneself, but the chances of a successful deer hunt go up sharply with the number of hunters. A deer is much more valuable than a hare. Then we have the kind of interaction that is now generally known as the stag hunt.

This chapter is drawn from my APA presidential address, Skyrms (2001).

Once you have formed this abstract representation of the stag hunt game, you can see stag hunts in many places. David Hume also has the stag hunt. His most famous illustration of a convention has the structure of a two-person stag hunt game: "Two men who pull at the oars of a boat, do it by an agreement or convention, tho' they have never given promises to each other."[2] Both men can either row or not row. If both row, they get the outcome that is best for each – just as, in Rousseau's example, when both hunt the stag. If one decides not to row, then it makes no difference if the other does or does not – they don't get anywhere. The worst outcome for you is if you row and the other doesn't, for then you lose your effort for nothing, just as the worst outcome for you in the stag hunt is if you hunt stag by yourself.

We meet the stag hunt again in the meadow-draining problem of Hume's *Treatise*: "Two neighbors may agree to drain a meadow, which they possess in common; because 'tis easy for them to know each others mind, and each may perceive that the immediate consequence of failing in his part is the abandoning of the whole project. But 'tis difficult, and indeed impossible, that a thousand persons shou'd agree in any such action."[3] In this brief passage, Hume displays a deep understanding of the essential issues involved. He sees that cooperation in the stag hunt is consistent with rationality. He sees that the viability of cooperation depends on mutual beliefs, and rests on trust. He observes that for these reasons, achieving cooperation in a many-person stag hunt is more difficult than achieving cooperation in a two-person stag hunt.[4]

The stag hunt does not have the same melodramatic quality as the prisoner's dilemma. It raises its own set of issues, which are at least as worthy of serious consideration. Let us focus, for the moment, on a two-person stag hunt for comparison to the familiar two-person prisoner's dilemma.

If two people cooperate in prisoner's dilemma, each is choosing less rather than more. In prisoner's dilemma, there is a conflict between individual rationality and mutual benefit. In the stag hunt, what is rational for one player to choose depends on his beliefs about what the other will choose. Both stag hunting and hare hunting are *Nash equilibria*. That is just to say that it is best to hunt stag if the other player hunts stag, and it is best to hunt hare if the other player hunts hare. A player who chooses to hunt stag takes a risk that the other will choose not to cooperate in the stag hunt. A player who chooses to hunt hare runs no such risk, since his payoff does not depend on the choice of action of the other player, but he forgoes the potential payoff of a successful stag hunt. In the stag hunt game, rational players are pulled in one direction by considerations of mutual benefit and in the other by considerations of personal risk.

Suppose that hunting hare has an expected payoff of 3, no matter what the other does. Hunting stag with another has an expected payoff of 4. Hunting stag alone is doomed to failure and has a payoff of 0. It is clear that a pessimist, who always expects the worst, would hunt hare. But it is also true with these payoffs that a cautious player, who was so uncertain that he thought the other player was as likely to do one thing as another, would also hunt hare. Hunting hare is said to be the *risk-dominant* equilibrium.[5] That is not to say that rational players could not coordinate on the stag hunt equilibrium that gives them both a better payoff, but it is to say that they need a measure of trust to do so.

I told the story so that the payoff of hunting hare is absolutely independent of how others act. We could vary this slightly without affecting the underlying theme. Perhaps if you hunt hare, it is even better for you if the other hunts stag, for you avoid competition for the hare. If the effect is small, we still have an interaction that is much like the Stag Hunt. It displays the same tension between risk and mutual benefit. It raises the same question of trust. This small variation on the stag hunt is sometimes also called a stag hunt,[6] and we will follow this more inclusive usage here.

Compared to the prisoner's dilemma, the stag hunt has received relatively little discussion in contemporary social philosophy – although there are some notable exceptions.[7] But I think that the stag hunt should be a focal point for social contract theory.

The two mentioned games, prisoner's dilemma and the stag hunt, are not unrelated. We will illustrate the connection in two rather different contexts – the first dealing with considerations of prudence, self-interest, and rational choice, and the second having to do with evolutionary dynamics in a model of group selection.

THE STAG HUNT AND THE SHADOW OF THE FUTURE

The first context arises in classical political philosophy. Considerations raised by both Hobbes and Hume can show that a seeming prisoner's dilemma is really a stag hunt. Suppose that prisoner's dilemma is repeated. Then your actions on one play may affect your partner's actions on other plays, and considerations of reputation may assume an importance that they cannot have if there is no repetition. Such considerations form the substance of Hobbes's reply to the Foole. Hobbes does not believe that the Foole has made a mistake concerning the nature of rational decision. Rather, he accuses the Foole of a shortsighted mis-specification of the relevant game: "He, therefore, that breaketh his Covenant, and consequently declareth that he think that he may with reason do so, cannot be received into any society that unite themselves for Peace and Defense, but by the error of them that receive him."[8] According to Hobbes, the Foole's mistake is to ignore the future.

David Hume invokes the same considerations in a more general setting: "Hence I learn to do a service to another, without bearing him any real kindness; because I foresee, that he will return my service, in expectation of another of the same kind, and in order to maintain the same correspondence of good offices with me and with others."[9] Hobbes and Hume are invoking the *shadow of the future*.[10]

How can we analyze the shadow of the future? We can use the theory of indefinitely repeated games. Suppose that the probability that the prisoner's dilemma will be repeated another time is constant. In the repeated game, the *Foole* has the strategy of always defecting. Hobbes argues that if someone defects, others will never cooperate with the defector. Those who initially cooperate but who retaliate, as Hobbes suggests against defectors, have a *Trigger* strategy.

If we suppose that Foole and Trigger are the only strategies available in the repeated game and that the probability of another trial is .6, then the shadow of the future transforms the two-person prisoner's dilemma

	Cooperate	Defect
Cooperate	2	0
Defect	3	1

into the two-person stag hunt.[11]

	Trigger	Foole
Trigger	5	1.5
Foole	4.5	2.5

This is an exact version of the informal arguments of Hume and Hobbes.[12]

But for the argument to be effective against a fool, he must believe that the others with whom he interacts are not fools. Those who play it safe will choose Foole. Rawls's maximin player is Hobbes's Foole.[13] The shadow of the future has not solved the problem of cooperation in the prisoner's dilemma; it has transformed it into the problem of cooperation in the stag hunt.

GROUP SELECTION AND THE STAG HUNT

Cooperation is also a problem for evolutionary theory. How can cooperation evolve in a context of competition for survival? Darwin recognized the problem. In Darwin's own time, it was the focus of Petr Kropotkin's 1908 *Mutual Aid: A Factor in Evolution*.

More recently (1962), V. C. Wynn-Edwards revived the issue in *Animal Dispersion in Relation to Social Behavior*. He argued that many natural populations practiced reproductive restraint, which is contrary to individual "selfish" behavior, because of its benefit to the group in preserving food supply. The idea was that natural selection applies to groups, as well as individuals. The explanatory force of this sort of appeal to "group selection" was severely criticized by George Williams in 1966. Natural selection operating on populations operates at a much slower rate than natural selection operating on individuals. Williams argued that as a result, group selection would be a much weaker evolutionary force than individual selection. After the publication of his *Adaptation and Natural Selection*, many evolutionary biologists dismissed group selection as an interesting part of evolutionary theory.

But John Maynard Smith, the father of evolutionary game theory, was motivated in 1964 to find a model in which some kind of group selection could account for the evolution of altruism. He took cooperation in the prisoner's dilemma as the paradigm of altruistic behavior.

Maynard Smith imagines a large hayfield. In the fall the farmer mows hay and makes haystacks. Each haystack is colonized by two mice, drawn at random, from the ambient mouse population. Over the winter the mice play prisoner's dilemma and reproduce. In the spring the haystacks are torn down, and the mice scatter to form the ambient population for the next cycle. Haystacks full of cooperative mice produce more mice than those full of defectors, so it seems that here the group structure – where inhabitants of a given haystack are the group – should be able to sustain the evolution of cooperation in the prisoner's dilemma.

We can see how this is so in the simplest possible haystack model. (There is a whole literature on generalized haystack models, and we will illustrate principles that hold good in general.) For simplicity we will suppose that the mice pair at random within the haystack, play the prisoner's dilemma, reproduce asexually with number of offspring determined by payoff, and repeat the process for the number of generations for which the haystack remains intact.

Consider the Prisoner's Dilemma.

	Cooperate	Defect
Cooperate	2	0
Defect	3	1

If the haystack is colonized by two defectors, each gets a payoff of 1, so in the next generation there are still two defectors, and so for all subsequent generations. If the haystack is founded by a defector and a cooperator, the cooperator gets a payoff of 0 and has no progeny. The defector gets a payoff of 3 and the next generation has three defectors. At all subsequent generations the haystack has only defectors, and so the population is maintained at 3 defectors. (Don't worry about pairing.) Two cooperators produce four cooperators in generation 1, eight in generation 2, and so forth.

If the haystacks are torn down after generation 1 is born, then group selection doesn't work. The dynamics is the same as if there were no group structure and defection drives out cooperation. But if the population stays together for two generations or more, it is possible for cooperation to be sustained.

There are two complementary ways to look at this result. One is to focus on the game played within the haystacks, the prisoner's dilemma. From this point of view, the key fact is that after one generation the dynamics induces perfect correlation of types – cooperators only meet cooperators and defectors only meet defectors. Then, of course, cooperators can flourish, because it is a defining characteristic of the prisoner's dilemma that cooperators do better against themselves than defectors do against defectors. The temporary advantage of being able to defect against cooperators is gone after the initial interaction because it removes potential victims from successive generations in the haystack.

The second way of looking at the haystack model, suggested by Ted Bergstrom in 2002, is to consider the game played by founders of the haystacks. Founders are chosen at random from the ambient population. The payoffs from the game between founders are the number of progeny when the haystack is torn down. In our example, if the haystacks are torn down after two generations, the payoffs in the founders game are as follows:

	Cooperate	Defect
Cooperate	4	0
Defect	3	1

This is a stag hunt.

And, as we know, the stag hunt does not *solve* the problem of cooperation. It allows cooperation in equilibrium, but there is also the noncooperative equilibrium. If we start our two-generation haystack dynamics in a state where the ambient population is equally divided between cooperators and defectors, defection will take over the population. Group selection can transform the problem of cooperation in the prisoner's dilemma into the problem of cooperation in the stag hunt.

THE STAG HUNT AND THE SOCIAL CONTRACT

In a larger sense, the whole problem of adopting or modifying the social contract for mutual benefit can be seen as a stag hunt. For a social contract theory to make sense, the state of nature must be an equilibrium. Otherwise, there would not be the problem of transcending it. And the state where the social contract has been adopted must also be an equilibrium. Otherwise, the social contract would not be viable. Suppose that you can either *devote energy to instituting the new social contract* or not. If everyone takes the first course, the social contract equilibrium is achieved; if everyone takes the second course, the state of nature equilibrium results. But the second course carries no risk, while the first does. This is all quite nicely illustrated in miniature by the meadow-draining problem of Hume.

The problem of reforming the social contract has the same structure. Here, following Ken Binmore (1993), we can then take the relevant "state of nature" to be the status quo, and the relevant social contract to be the projected reform. The problem of instituting, or improving, the social contract can be thought of as the problem of moving from riskless hunt hare equilibrium to the risky but rewarding stag hunt equilibrium.

9

GAME DYNAMICS

How do we get from the hunt hare equilibrium to the stag hunt equilibrium? We could approach the problem in two different ways. We could follow Hobbes in asking the question in terms of rational self-interest. Or we could follow Hume by asking the question in a dynamic setting. We can ask these questions using modern tools – which are more than Hobbes and Hume had available, but still less than we need for fully adequate answers.

The modern embodiment of Hobbes's approach is rational choice–based game theory. It tells us that what a rational player will do in the stag hunt depends on what that player thinks the other will do. It agrees with Hume's contention that a thousand-person stag hunt would be more difficult to achieve than a two-person stag hunt, because – assuming that everyone must cooperate for a successful outcome to the hunt – the problem of trust is multiplied. But if we ask how people can get from a hare hunt equilibrium to a stag hunt equilibrium, it does not have much to offer. From the standpoint of rational choice, for the hare hunters to decide to be stag hunters, each must *change individual beliefs* about what the other will do. But rational choice–based game theory, as usually conceived, has nothing to say about how or why such a change of mind might take place.

Let us turn to the tradition of Hume. Hume emphasized that social norms can evolve slowly: "Nor is the rule regarding the stability of possession the less derived from human conventions, that it arises gradually, and acquires force by a slow progression."[14] We can reframe our problem in terms of the most thoroughly studied model of cultural evolution, the replicator dynamics.[15] This is a deterministic dynamics, intended for large populations in which the effects of chance fluctuations average out. We can ask, in this framework, how one can get

10

from the hunt hare equilibrium to the hunt stag equilibrium; the answer is that you can't! In the vicinity of the state where all hunt hare, hunting hare has the greatest payoff. If you are close to it, the dynamics carries you back to it.

This reasoning holds good over a large class of adaptive deterministic dynamics, which generalize the replicator dynamics. Let us say that a dynamics is *adaptive* if it leads to strategies that do better than average increasing their population proportion and to strategies that do worse than average decreasing their population proportion. For any adaptive dynamics, the reasoning of the previous paragraph continues to hold good. The transition from noncooperation to cooperation seems impossible.

Perhaps the restriction to deterministic dynamics is the problem. We may just need to add some chance variation. We could add some chance shocks to the replicator dynamics[16] or look at a finite population where people have some chance of doing the wrong thing, or just experimenting to see what will happen.[17] If we wait long enough, chance variation will bounce the population out of hare hunting and into stag hunting. But in the same way, chance variation can bounce the population out of stag hunting into hare hunting. Can we say anything more than that the population bounces between these two states?

We can,[18] and in this case the analysis is very simple. It depends on the relative magnitude of the basins of attraction of the stag hunting equilibrium and the hare hunting equilibrium. Let me illustrate with our original version of the stag hunt game: Hunting hare has a payoff of 3, no matter what the other does; hunting stag with another has a payoff of 4; and hunting stag alone has a payoff of 0. If more than 75 percent of the population hunts stag, then stag hunters will take over. This is the "basin of attraction" of the stag hunting equilibrium. If less than 75 percent of the population hunts stag, then hare hunters will take over. This is the basin of attraction of the hare hunting equilibrium – which is triple the size of that of the stag hunting equilibrium.

If mutation (or experimentation) probabilities are small and independent across individuals, and the population is large, it will be much more likely for chance events to move the population from the stag hunting equilibrium into the basin of attraction of hare hunting than for the converse to happen. In the long run, the population spends almost all of its time in a state where everyone hunts hare.[19] It seems that all we have achieved so far is to show how the social contract might degenerate spontaneously into the state of nature.

Social contracts do sometimes spontaneously dissolve. But social contracts also form. People do, in fact, engage in stag hunts (and antelope hunts and giraffe hunts and pig hunts and bison hunts). Cooperative hunting is an ancient part of the human social contract that goes back to the beginning of our race. It is not so easy to infer those distant payoffs and to determine the risk-dominant equilibrium in an appropriate game model. But there is contemporary experimental evidence that people will sometimes hunt stag even when it is a risk to do so.[20] In a whole series of experiments, stag hunting is the most frequent strategy on the first round. People do not enter the laboratory with a norm of playing the risk-dominant strategy. When the game is repeated with pairwise random matching in a group of subjects, sometimes the group converges to all stag hunting and sometimes to all hare hunting, depending on the initial composition of the group. If the group starts in the basin of attraction of stag hunting, then the group almost always converges to all stag hunters. If the initial composition of the group is in the basin of attraction of hare hunting, hare hunters take over.

In a novel experiment, F. W. Rankin, J. B. Van Huyck, and R. Battalio presented subjects with a series of stag hunts in which payoffs varied from game to game and action labels were changed, so that subjects needed to evolve some rule for deal-ing with them. Subjects converged to payoff – dominance. Stag hunting, although it was not identified as such to the subjects, emerged as a coordination principle.[21] These experimental re-sults, as well as our wider knowledge of the world of social interactions, suggest the need for a richer theory.

PART I

LOCATION

ONE strain of *E. coli* bacteria produces a poison, to which it is immune, that kills competing strains. It takes resources to produce the poison, and the strain that produces it pays a cost in reproduction for the privilege of killing competitors. If the poisoner strain evolved from a more peaceful strain of *E. coli*, how did it get started? According to the large-population, random-encounter model discussed in Chapter 1, it can't. A few mutant poisoners would cause little change to the average fitness of a large peaceful group. They would nevertheless bear the cost of producing the poison, and so have lower average fitness than the natives. Theory is confirmed in the laboratory. If a few mutant poisoners are added to a well-stirred culture of peaceful *E. coli*, the mutants are gradually eliminated.

But when the same experiment is performed on agar plates rather than in a well-stirred solution, the poisoners can invade and eventually take over the population.[1] Here theory followed experiment, and theoretical treatments of the local interaction involved also followed, providing analytic explanations of the experimental results.[2] I won't tell the full story here, but I hope that I have told enough to illustrate the importance of spatial structure, location, and local interaction for evolutionary dynamics.

Another illustration, in a rosier hue, comes from the effect of spatial structure on the evolution of cooperation in prisoner's dilemma games. If prisoner's dilemmas are played in a well-mixed large population, the evolutionary dynamics drives cooperation to extinction. But a number of different investigators have shown how interaction with neighbors on one or another spatial structure can allow cooperative strategies to persist in the population.[3] In some cases, the population displays very complicated dynamics that never settle into an equilibrium. The basic idea is not exactly new. Biologists, notably William Hamilton and John Maynard Smith,[4] have emphasized spatial structure as an important factor in the evolution of cooperation. But recently there has been a flowering of precise models and analyses of evolution driven by local interaction on spatial structures.

Local interaction may have something important to teach us about the dynamics of the social contract and, in particular, about the dynamics of the stag hunt.

2

BARGAINING WITH NEIGHBORS

JUSTICE

WHAT is justice? The question is harder to answer in some cases than in others. Philosophers usually like to discuss the hard cases, in which disagreement is inevitable. Here we will focus on the easiest case of distributive justice. Two individuals are to decide how to distribute a windfall of a certain amount of money. Neither is especially entitled, or especially needy, or especially anything – their positions are entirely symmetric. Their utilities derived from the distribution may, for all intents and purposes, be taken simply as the amount of money received. If they cannot decide, the money remains undistributed and neither gets any. The essence of the situation is captured in the simplest version of a bargaining game devised by John Nash in 1950. Each person decides on a bottom-line demand. If those demands do not jointly exceed the windfall, then each person gets his or her demand; if not, no one gets anything. This game is often simply called "divide-the-dollar." One can imagine countless other bargaining games, but for the moment we examine the evolutionary dynamics of this one.

This chapter is largely drawn from Alexander and Skyrms (1999).

In the ideal simple case, the question of distributive justice can be decided by two principles:

Optimality: A distribution is not just if under an alternative distribution all recipients would be better off.

Equity: If the position of the recipients is symmetric, then the distribution should be symmetric. That is to say, it does not vary when we switch the recipients.

Since we stipulate that the position of the two individuals is symmetric, equity requires that the just distribution must give them the same amount of money. Optimality then rules out such unlikely schemes as giving each one a dime and throwing the rest away – each must get half the money.

There is nothing new about our two principles. Equity is the simplest consequence of the theory of distributive justice in Aristotle's *Politics*. It is a consequence of Kant's categorical imperative. Utilitarians tend to stress optimality, but are not completely insensitive to equity. Optimality and equity are the two most uncontroversial requirements in John Nash's axiomatic treatment of bargaining. They are shared by axiomatic treatments, such as that of E. Kalai and M. Smordinski (1975), which disagree with Nash's theory in less symmetric bargaining situations, but agree with Nash in divide-the-dollar.

In a famous series of experiments, Menachem Yaari and Maya Bar-Hillel (1981) asked people to judge the just distribution of goods in hypothetical circumstances. Their answers show that optimality and equity are powerful operative principles. Disagreements arose in those cases in which these principles could be applied in more that one way. We have carefully circumscribed our bargaining problem so that the application of the principles is unambiguous. The equal split in divide-the-dollar is the least controversial example that we have of dividing justly.

RATIONALITY

Two rational agents play the divide-the-dollar game. Their rationality is common knowledge. What do they do? *Any* combination of demands is compatible with these assumptions. For example, Jack may demand 90 percent thinking that Jill will only demand 10 percent on the assumption that Jill thinks that Jack will demand 90 percent and so forth, while Jill demands 75 percent thinking that Jack will demand 25 percent on the assumption that Jack thinks that Jill will demand 75 percent and so forth. *Any* pair of demands is *rationalizable*, in that it can be supported by a hierarchy of conjectures for each player, compatible with common knowledge of rationality. In the example given, these conjectures are quite mistaken.

Suppose we add the assumption that each agent somehow knows what the other will demand. Then any combination of demands that total the whole sum to be divided is still possible. For example, suppose that Jack demands 90 percent knowing that Jill will demand 10 percent, and Jill demands 10 percent knowing that Jack will demand 90 percent. Then each player is maximizing payoff given the demand of the other. That is to say that this is a *Nash equilibrium* of divide-the-dollar. If the dollar were infinitely divisible, then there would be an infinite number of such equilibria.

Experimental game theorists operating in a laboratory can control the situation so as to approach the ideal symmetry demanded by our specification of divide-the-dollar. If experimental game theorists have people actually play divide-the-dollar, they *always* split equally.[1] This is not true in more complicated bargaining experiments where there are salient asymmetries, but it is true in divide-the-dollar. Rational choice theory has no explanation of this phenomenon. It appears that the experimental subjects are using norms of justice to select a particular Nash equilibrium of the game. But what account can we give for the existence of these norms?

Evolutionary game theory (reading "evolution" as cultural evolution) promises an explanation, but the promise is only partially fulfilled. Robert Sugden (1986) pointed out that demand-half is the only evolutionarily stable strategy in divide-the-dollar. That is to say that it is the only strategy such that if the whole population played that strategy, no small group of innovators, or "mutants," playing a different strategy could achieve an average payoff at least as great as that of the natives. If we could be sure that this unique evolutionarily stable strategy would always take over the population, the problem would be solved.

But we cannot be sure that this will happen. Sugden also showed that there are states of the population where some fraction of the population makes one demand and some fraction makes another that are evolutionarily stable. The state where half the population demands one-third and half the population demands two-thirds is such an evolutionarily stable polymorphism of the population. So is the state where two-thirds of the population demands 40 percent and one-third of the population demands 60 percent. We can think of these as pitfalls along the evolutionary road to justice.

How important are these polymorphisms? To what extent do they compromise the evolutionary explanation of the egalitarian norm? We cannot begin to answer these questions without explicitly modeling the evolutionary dynamics and investigating the size of their basins of attraction.

BARGAINING WITH STRANGERS

The dynamic evolutionary model of Chapter 1 is a model of interactions with strangers. Suppose that individuals are paired at random from a very large population to play the bargaining

20

game. We assume that the probability of meeting a strategy can be taken as the proportion of the population that has that strategy. The population proportions evolve according to the replicator dynamics. The proportion of the population using a strategy in the next generation is the proportion playing that strategy in the current generation multiplied by a "fitness factor." This fitness factor is just the ratio of the average payoff to this strategy to the average payoff in the whole population.[2] Strategies that do better than average grow; those that do worse than average shrink. This dynamics arose in biology as a model of asexual reproduction, but more to the point here, it also has a cultural evolutionary interpretation where strategies are imitated in proportion to their success.[3]

The basins of attraction of these polymorphic pitfalls are not negligible. A realistic version of divide-the-dollar will have some finite number of strategies instead of the infinite number that we get from the idealization of infinite divisibility. For a finite number of strategies, the size of a basin of attraction of a population state makes straightforward sense. It can be estimated by computer simulations. We can consider coarse-grained or fine-grained versions of divide-the-dollar; we can divide a stack of quarters, or of dimes, or of pennies. Some results of simulations persist across a range of different granularities. Equal division always has the largest basin of attraction, and it is always greater than the basins of attractions of all the polymorphic pitfalls combined. If you choose an initial population state at random, it is more probable than not that the replicator dynamics will converge to a state of fixation of demand-half. Simulation results range between 57 and 63 percent of the initial points going to fair division. The next largest basin of attraction is always that closest to the equal split – for example, the 4–6 polymorphism in the case of dividing a stack of ten dimes and the 49–51 polymorphism in the case of dividing a stack of a hundred pennies. The rest of the polymorphic

Table 2.1. Convergence
Results for Replicator
Dynamics – 100,000 Trials

Fair Division	62,209
4–6 Polymorphism	27,469
3–7 Polymorphism	8,801
2–8 Polymorphism	1,483
1–9 Polymorphism	38
0–10 Polymorphism	0

equilibria follow the general rule – the closer to fair division, the larger the basin of attraction.

For example, the results running the discrete replicator dynamics to convergence and repeating the process 100,000 times on the game of dividing ten dimes are given in Table 2.1. The projected evolutionary explanation seems to fall somewhat short. The best we might say on the basis of pure replicator dynamics is that fixation of fair division is more likely that not, and that polymorphisms far from fair division are quite unlikely.

We can say something more if we inject a little bit of probability into the model. Suppose that every once in a while a member of the population just picks a strategy at random and tries it out – perhaps as an experiment, perhaps just as a mistake. Suppose we are at a polymorphic equilibrium, for instance the 4–6 equilibrium in the problem of dividing ten dimes. If there is some fixed probability of an experiment (or mistake), and if experiments are independent, and if we wait long enough, there will be enough experiments of the right kind to kick the population out of the basin of attraction of the 4–6 polymorphism and into the basin of attraction of fair division, and the evolutionary dynamics will carry fair division to fixation. Eventually, experiments or mistakes will kick the population out of the basin of attraction of fair division, but we should expect to wait much longer for this to happen. In the long run, the system will spend most of its time in the fair division equilibrium. Peyton Young showed that in the limit, as the probability of someone experimenting approaches zero, the ratio of time spent in fair division approaches one. In his terminology, fair division is the unique *stochastically stable equilibrium* of this bargaining game.[4] We see that this setting is much more favorable to fair division in the bargaining game than to stag hunting. As noted in Chapter 1, the unique stochastically stable equilibrium in the stag hunt game is the equilibrium where everyone hunts hare.

This explanation gets us a probability arbitrarily close to one of finding a fair division equilibrium if we are willing to wait an arbitrarily long time. But how long are we willing to wait? Ask yourself how long you would expect it to take in a population of 10,000, for 1,334 demand-6 types to simultaneously try out being demand-5 types and thus kick the population out of the basin of attraction of the 4–6 polymorphism and into the basin of attraction of fair division.[5] The evolutionary explanation still seems less than compelling.

BARGAINING WITH NEIGHBORS

The model of random encounters in an infinite population that motivates the replicator dynamics may not be the right model. Suppose interactions are with neighbors. Jason McKenzie Alexander[6] investigated a population of 10,000 arranged on a 100-by-100 square lattice. As the neighbors of an individual in the interior of the lattice, we take the eight individuals to the N, NE, E, SE, S, SW, W, NW. This is called the Moore (8) neighborhood in the cellular automaton literature. (Results were not much different if only N,S,E,W, the von Neumann (4) neighborhood, was used.) The dynamics is driven by imitation. Individuals imitate the most successful person in the neighborhood. A generation – an iteration of the discrete dynamics – has two stages. First, each individual plays the divide-ten-dimes game with each of her neighbors, using her current strategy. Summing the payoffs gives her current success level. Then, each player looks around her neighborhood and changes her current strategy by imitating her most successful neighbor, providing that her most successful neighbor is more successful than she is. Otherwise, she does not switch strategies. (Ties are broken by a coin flip.)

In initial trials of this model, fair division *always* went to fixation. This cannot quite be a universal law, since you can design "rigged" configurations where a few demand-$\frac{1}{2}$ players are so situated that demand-$\frac{1}{2}$ will disappear.[7] Start enough simulations at random starting points and sooner or later you will start at one of these. To determine the magnitude of the neighbor effect, a·large simulation was run starting repeatedly at randomly chosen starting points. Fair division went to fixation in more that 99.5 percent of the trials. The cases where it didn't were all cases where the initial population of 10,000 contained fewer than seventeen demand-$\frac{1}{2}$ players. Furthermore, convergence was remarkably quick. Mean time to fixation of fair division was about sixteen generations. This may be compared with a mean time to convergence[8] in discrete replicator dynamics of forty-six generations, and with the ultra-long-run character of stochastically stable equilibrium.

It is possible to exclude fair division from the possible initial strategies in the divide-ten-dimes game and start at random starting points that include the rest. If we do this, all strategies other than demand-4 dimes and demand-6 dimes are eliminated and the 4–6 polymorphic population falls into a "blinking" cycle of period 2. If we then turn on a little bit of random experimentation or "mutation" allowing the possibility

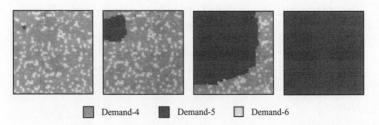

Demand-4 Demand-5 Demand-6

Figure 2.1. The Steady Advance of Fair Division

of demand-5, we find that as soon as a very small clump of demand-5 players arises, it systematically grows until it takes over the whole population, as illustrated in Figure 2.1. *Justice is contagious.*

ROBUSTNESS

The bargaining-with-neighbors model of the last section differs from the bargaining-with-strangers model in more than one way. Might the difference in behavior that we have just described be due to the imitate-the-most-successful dynamics, rather than the neighbor effect? To answer this question we ran simulations varying these factors independently.

We consider both fixed and random neighborhoods. The models using fixed neighborhoods use the Moore (8) neighborhood described in the previous section. In the alternative random neighborhood model, each generation a new set of "neighbors" is chosen at random from the population for each individual. That is to say, these are neighborhoods of *strangers*.

We investigated two alternative dynamics. One imitates the most successful neighbor as in our bargaining-with-neighbors model. The other tempers the all-or-nothing character of imitate-the-best. Under it, an individual imitates one of the strategies in its neighborhood that is more successful than it (if

Table 2.2. Convergence Results for Five Series of
10,000 Trials

	Bargaining with Neighbors		Bargaining with Strangers	
	A	B	C	D
0–10	0	0	0	0
1–9	0	0	0	0
2–8	0	0	54	57
3–7	0	0	550	556
4–6	26	26	2560	2418
Fair	9,972	9,973	6,833	6,964

there are any), with relative probability proportional to their success in the neighborhood. This is a move in the direction of the replicator dynamics. The results are shown in Table 2.2. In this table, Columns A and B are bargaining with neighbors, with imitate-the-best-neighbor and imitate-with-probability-proportional-to-success dynamics, respectively. The results are barely distinguishable. Columns C and D are the random neighborhood models corresponding to A and B, respectively. These results are much closer to those given for the replicator dynamics in Table 2.1. The dramatic difference in convergence to fair division between our two models is due to the structure of interaction with neighbors.

ANALYSIS

Why is justice contagious? A strategy is contagious if an initial "patch" of that strategy will extend to larger and larger patches. The key to contagion of a strategy is interaction along the edges of the patch, since in the interior the strategy can only imitate itself.[9]

26

Consider an edge with demand-5 players on one side, and players playing the complementary strategies of one of the polymorphisms on the other. Since the second ranks of demand-5 players always meet their own kind, they each get a total payoff of 40 from their eight neighbors. Players in the first rank will therefore imitate them unless a neighbor from the polymorphism gets a higher payoff. The low strategy in a polymorphic pair cannot get a higher payoff. So if demand-5 is to be replaced at all, it must be by the high strategy of one of the polymorphic pairs.

In the 4–6 polymorphism – the polymorphism with the greatest basin of attraction in the replicator dynamics – this simply cannot happen, even in the most favorable circumstances. Suppose that we have someone playing demand-6 in the first rank of the polymorphism, surrounded on his own side by compatible demand-4 players to boost his payoff to the maximum possible.[10] Since he is in the first rank, he faces three incompatible demand-5 neighbors. He has a total payoff of 30, while his demand-5 neighbors have a total payoff of 35. Demand-5 begins an inexorable march forward, as illustrated in Figure 2.2. (The pattern is assumed to extend in all directions for the computation of payoffs of players at the periphery of what is shown in the figure.)

If we choose a polymorphism that is more extreme, however, it is possible for the high strategy to replace some demand-5 players for a while. Consider the 1–9 polymorphism, with a

Initial		Iteration 1
5544		5554
5544		5554
5564	=>	5554
5544		5554
5544		5554

Figure 2.2. Fair Division vs. 4–6 Polymorphism

Initial		Iteration 1		Iteration 2		Iteration 3
55*111*		555*11*		5555*1*		55555
55*111*		555*11*		5555*9*		5555*9*
55*111*	=>	5*9991*	=>	55*999*	=>	555*99*
55*911*		5*9991*		55*999*		555*99*
55*111*		5*9991*		55*999*		555*99*
55*111*		555*11*		5555*9*		5555*9*
55*111*		555*11*		5555*1*		55555

Figure 2.3. Fair Division vs. 1–9 Polymorphism

front line demand-9 player backed by compatible demand-1 neighbors. The demand-9 player gets a total payoff of 45 – more than anyone else – and thus is imitated by all his neighbors. This is shown in the first transition in Figure 2.3. But the success of the demand-9 strategy is its own undoing. In a cluster of demand-9 strategies, it meets itself too often and does not do so well. In the second transition, demand-5 has more than regained its lost territory, and in the third transition, it has solidly advanced into 1–9 territory.

The interaction along an edge between demand-5 and other polymorphisms is similar to one of the two cases analyzed here.[11] Either the polymorphism cannot advance at all, or the advance creates the conditions for its immediate reversal.

CONCLUSION

Sometimes we bargain with neighbors, sometimes with strangers. The dynamics of the two sorts of interaction are quite different. In the bargaining game considered here, bargaining with strangers – modeled by the replicator dynamics – leads to fair division from a randomly chosen starting point about 60 percent of the time. Fair division becomes the unique answer in bargaining with strangers if we change the question to that of stochastic stability in the ultra long run. But long expected waiting times call the explanatory significance of the stochastic stability result into question.

Bargaining with neighbors almost always converges to fair division, and convergence is remarkably rapid. In bargaining with neighbors, the local interaction generates clusters of those strategies that are locally successful. Clustering and local interaction together produce positive correlation between like strategies. As noted elsewhere,[12] positive correlation favors fair division over the polymorphisms. In bargaining with neighbors, this positive correlation is not something externally imposed but, rather, an unavoidable consequence of the dynamics of local interaction. As a consequence, once a small group of demand-half players is formed, justice becomes contagious and rapidly takes over the entire population.

3

STAG HUNT WITH NEIGHBORS

L OCAL interaction gave us an account of how the convention of the equal split can invade a population stuck in
an inefficient and inequitable polymorphism of the bargaining
game, and spread to take over the entire population. Is local
interaction the key we seek for enabling the transition from
the hare hunting equilibrium to the stag hunting equilibrium
in the stag hunt game?

THE BAD NEWS

In 1993, Glenn Ellison investigated the dynamics of the stag
hunt played with neighbors, where the players are arranged
on a circle. He found limiting behavior not much different from
that in the large population with random encounters. With a
small chance of error, the population spends most of its time in
the risk-dominant equilibrium – which in our stag hunt games
is hunting hare.

The difference in the dynamics between the large population
with random encounters and the small population with local
interaction is that in the latter, the population approaches its
long-run behavior much more rapidly. *Hare hunting is contagious.*
The moral for us, if any, seems to be that in small groups with

local interaction, the degeneration of the social contract into the state of nature can occur with great rapidity.

But let us not be too hasty in swallowing that moral. Consider the dynamics of the stag hunt game played on a lattice under exactly the same assumptions as those used in the previous chapter to investigate bargaining on a lattice. An individual is either a stag hunter or a hare hunter. She plays the stag hunt game with her neighbors to the N, NE, E, SE, S, SW, W, NW – the Moore (8) neighborhood – on a 100-by-100 square lattice. Then if she has a neighbor with a total payoff greater than hers, she changes her strategy by imitating the neighbor with the highest total payoff (ties broken by a coin flip). Otherwise, she keeps the same strategy.

We focus on our prototypical stag hunt, where hare hunters always get 2, and stag hunters get 3 if they work with another stag hunter and 0 if they work with a hare hunter. For comparison, we know from Chapter 1 that if a large, random mixing population were started with 50 percent stag hunters and 50 percent hare hunters, the replicator dynamics converges to a population where all hunt hare.

What happens when we run our imitate-the-best-neighbor, Moore (8), dynamics on our 100-by-100 lattice, initialized with 50 percent stag hunters and 50 percent hare hunters? There are many lattice configurations that answer to this description, so we need to average over them to make a comparison. We pick one at random, let it run to equilibrium, repeat the process, and keep track of the averages. If we do this, we get a pleasant surprise. *Stag hunters take over the population in about 99 percent of the trials.* If we observe the evolution of the population, it as apparent that wherever there are jagged edges between stag hunters and hare hunters, or a rectangle of hare hunters surrounded by stag hunters, the stag hunters march forward. Here it is stag hunting rather than hare hunting that is contagious (or semi-contagious).

How do we reconcile the seemingly contradictory bad news and good news? Is it hare hunting or stag hunting that is contagious? We must take a closer look at the respective local interaction models, and the dynamics that drive them.

TWO KINDS OF DYNAMICS

The good-news dynamics was *imitate-the-best*, which we had already used in the last chapter. This is the simplest representative of a class of imitation dynamics that have been used as models for cultural evolution. Similar dynamics arose in models of biological evolution. Imitation with probability proportional to success, when applied to a large population with random encounters, gives us the replicator dynamics, which was originally proposed as a model of differential reproduction. Whether success is proportional to biological offspring and strategies are inherited, or success is proportional to "offspring by imitation" where strategies are chosen, the underlying dynamics is the same. As a class we can think of these imitation-based dynamics as Darwinian in character.

The bad news from Ellison's model was generated by a different dynamical rule, *best response against your neighbors*. An individual looks at what his neighbors did last time, assumes that they will do the same this time, and picks the strategy that, when played against all the neighbors, will give the highest payoff in the current interaction. Put this way, best response against neighbors seems a little odd. If you are self-conscious enough to make a prediction and decide on the basis of your self-interest on the basis of that prediction, then shouldn't you be sufficiently calculating as to play different strategies against different neighbors if that appears optimal? If one of my neighbors is a stag hunter and the other a hare hunter, shouldn't I hunt stag with the stag hunter and hare with the hare hunter?

A different scenario can make the dynamics more plausible. You won't really have an interaction with each of your neighbors. One of your neighbors will be picked at random, and you will have an interaction with that person. Since each neighbor has an equal chance of being the one with whom you interact, picking the action that maximizes your expected payoff is the same as picking the action that, if played against all of your neighbors, maximizes your payoff.

Viewed in this way, best response against your neighbors is the simplest representative of a class of rules that tries to predict what situation you are about to face on the basis of past experience, and chooses the strategy that optimizes current payoff on the basis of that prediction. All these rules are shortsighted, in that they do not try to take into account the effect of your present act on others' future acts. They are blind to the shadow of the future. But they are somewhat more calculating than Darwinian strategy revision. Best response is a stripped-down version of rational choice. It is rational choice coupled with a simple-minded predictive rule and a naive view of consequences.

Is this minimal form of rational choice the obstacle to cooperation in Ellison's model? Is it Darwinian dynamics that promotes stag hunting in Alexander's model? Or are other factors that differ between the two models responsible for the change from bad news to good?

A CLOSER LOOK AT THE MODELS

The bad news came from Ellison's one-dimensional model of interaction with neighbors on a circle. The dynamics is to choose the action that is best response when played against each of the actions your neighbors played last time. The good news came from Alexander's two-dimensional model of interaction with (8) neighbors on a square lattice. The dynamics is to imitate the neighbor who was most successful overall the last time (or to imitate the most successful strategy in the neighborhood, or to imitate neighborhood strategies with probability proportional to success). Both the dimensionalities of the models and the dynamic rule that governs evolution of the population differ.

Consider our stag hunt played with immediate neighbors on a circle with best response dynamics. Each individual has two neighbors. Either both hunt stag, both hunt hare, or there is one of each strategy. If both an individual's neighbors hunt stag, then her best response is to hunt stag, and that is what she does next time. Likewise, if both neighbors of an individual hunt hare, then she best responds by hunting hare. If there is one hare hunting neighbor and one stag hunting neighbor, then she must choose a strategy that is the best response on average – the one that maximizes $\frac{1}{2}$ (payoff against stag hunter) $+ \frac{1}{2}$ (payoff against hare hunter). In this case, hare hunting, with an average payoff of 2, beats stag hunting with an average payoff of $1\frac{1}{2}$. (We recall from Chapter 1 that this is just the feature that set up the conflict between considerations of mutual benefit and individual risk that we found so interesting in the stag hunt game.) She best responds to mixed neighbors by hunting hare. These facts completely characterize the dynamics of stag hunt on a circle.

Suppose that everyone hunts hare, and a mutant stag hunter pops up somewhere. Next time, the stag hunter switches to hunting hare because both his neighbors did, and his neighbors hunt hare because *they* had mixed neighbors, and everyone else hunts hare because everyone else had hare hunters on both sides. The population is restored to everyone hunting hare. The hare hunting equilibrium is stable. What about the equilibrium where everyone is hunting stag and one mutant hare hunter pops up? The mutant hare hunter switches to stag

```
     H        S        H        S
   S S  =>  H H  =>  S S    => H H
   S S      S S      H H   <= S S
     S        S        S        H
```

Figure 3.1. Hare Hunters Invade

hunting next time because both his neighbors hunted stag, but his neighbors both switch to hunting hare because *they* had mixed neighbors. At the time after that, these switch to hunting stag, but *their* neighbors switch to hunting hare. For an even number of players, this process leads to a cycle. In Figure 3.1 it is illustrated for a population of six players. Evidently All Hunt Stag is not stable in the way that All Hunt Hare is.

While the population is in the cycle, a new mutant hare hunter may pop up such that there are two contiguous hare hunters. If there are two continuous hare hunters in any size population, then hare hunting takes over the entire population. Two contiguous hare hunters never switch because at worst they are surrounded by stag hunters, they have mixed neighbors, and they remain hare hunters. And stag hunters that are their neighbors do switch to hare hunting (because such stag hunters have mixed neighbors). In this way, the hare hunters march forward, converting stag hunters they encounter along the way, until the entire population is composed of hare hunters. Hare hunting is contagious.

It is worth noting here that exactly the kind of interaction structure just described has been used for experiments in the economics laboratory. Eight subjects are arranged in a circle, by computer networking, and play the stag hunt with immediate neighbors.[1] Cycles never are observed, and observations of repeated trials are to some extent at variance with the best-reply dynamics. Observed convergence is not faster with local interaction than with random pairing in a group of the same size. Some groups converge to all hunting stag under local interaction, although more converge to all hunting hare. The experimental results suggest that the model be taken with a grain of salt.

The advantages that stag hunting obtains on a two-dimensional lattice with imitate-the-best dynamics are not quite so dramatic. Simulations show that if we start out with 50 percent or more stag hunters, we almost always end up with a population of all stag hunters. If we start with 10 percent stag hunters, we almost always end up with a population of all hare hunters. Both these states are stable. A mutant hare hunter immediately converts to stag hunting in a population of stag hunters, just as a mutant stag hunter converts to hare hunting in a population of hare hunters.

But if we start with 30 or 40 percent stag hunters, we frequently arrive at equilibrium states that consist of one or more rectangles of stag hunters surrounded by hare hunters. Why are these equilibrium configurations? It is easy to see that edges between two populations are stable. Consider the boldface stag and hare hunters in Figure 3.2.

All hare hunters get a payoff of 16 [2 for each Moore (8) neighbor]. The leading-edge stag hunter gets a payoff of 15 [3 for each stag hunter he meets]. The hare hunter keeps her strategy because all she sees are leading-edge stag hunters and other hare hunters. The stag hunter sees non-leading-edge stag hunters to his NW, W, and SW, and they all get a payoff of 24 because they meet only other stag hunters. The stag hunter imitates these interior stag hunters, and remains a stag hunter.

SSSHHH
SSSHHH
SS**SH**HH
SSSHHH
SSSHHH

Figure 3.2. Edges

Location

```
      SSS
      SSS
    HHHSS
    HHH
    HHH
```

Figure 3.3. Corner

```
SSSSSS        SSSSSS        SSSSSS
HHHSSS   =>   HHSSSS   =>   HSSSSS   =>
HHHSSS        HHHSSS        HHSSSS
HHHSSS        HHHSSS        HHHSSS
```

Figure 3.4. Stag Hunters Advance on the Diagonal

The corners of the rectangle remain unchanged for the same reason. The corner stag hunter imitates prosperous interior stag hunters. The hare hunters see no interior stag hunters and do not change.

A rectangle of hare hunters surrounded by stag hunters does not do so well. A corner hare hunter sees a stag hunter who interacts with him and seven other stag hunters and converts to stag hunting, as shown in Figure 3.3. This leads to further conversions that destroy the group of hare hunters, as shown in Figure 3.4.

In a ragged diagonal edge between the two groups, all the leading-edge hare hunters can see prosperous interior stag hunters that meet six or seven other stag hunters, and that get a greater payoff than any hare hunter. This accounts for the semi-contagious advance of stag hunters remarked on earlier. This breakdown of rectangles of hare hunters also happens if we change the imitation dynamics from the more easily analyzed "imitate the best individual in the neighborhood" to the more realistic "imitate the strategy that performs best on average in the neighborhood."

38

If we use the same dynamics on the von Neumann (4) and the Moore (24) neighborhoods, it is still true that with $\frac{50}{50}$ initial population proportions, the stag hunt takes over more often, but the mechanisms involved in each case are a little different. Furthermore, the results are sensitive to the particular payoffs used. This suggests that the grain of salt recommended in the last section is also appropriate here.

DIMENSIONS AND DYNAMICS

We have two models that differ both in dimension and dynamics, best-response dynamics in one dimension and imitate-the-best dynamics in two dimensions. It is natural to ask what happens in the other two possibilities, keeping everything but dimension and dynamics fixed.

Is hare hunting still contagious under best-response dynamics in two dimensions? In a later paper, Ellison investigates the question on a two-dimensional lattice using the von Neumann (4) neighborhood. Hare hunting is no longer contagious! But it is still easier for a series of mutations to take one on a path that leads from the stag hunting equilibrium to the hare hunting equilibrium than to take one on a path in the opposite direction. Ellison is then able to show how rare mutations lead the system to spend most of its time hunting hare.

Does stag hunting take over in one dimension with imitate-the-best dynamics? The quasi-contagion that depended on the diagonal in two dimensions is lost. Consider the frontier between a group of stag hunters and a group of hare hunters in Figure 3.5. Everyone has two neighbors. All hare hunters get a total payoff of 4. The leading-edge stag hunter gets a total

SSSHH

Figure 3.5. One-Dimensional Frontier

payoff of 3, but he sees an interior stag hunter who gets a payoff of 6. The boundary remains unchanged. Hare hunters are not converted because they cannot see interior stag hunters, as they can in our two-dimensional model.

But is this a plausible restriction to build into imitation dynamics? We might want to consider situations where players can see interactions other than those in which they directly participate. One way to do this, suggested by I. Eshel, E. Sansome, and A. Shaked, is to introduce two neighborhoods – an *interaction neighborhood* and an *imitation neighborhood*. An individual plays the game with all neighbors in the interaction neighborhood, and imitates the best strategy in the imitation neighborhood. If we let the players see a bit further, but allowing a larger imitation neighborhood, then the somewhat ambiguous benefits of local interaction for stag hunting become much more well defined and robust.

In the foregoing example of the stag hunt on the line or the circle, if we let the imitation neighborhood extend two players in either direction (while the interaction neighborhood is confined to nearest neighbors), the contagion is restored. A group of three or more contiguous stag hunters spreads and takes over the population. (This is true for both imitate-the-best-neighbor and imitate-the-best-strategy in the neighborhood.)

Dimension, dynamics, and the kinds of neighborhoods involved all play a role in determining the outcome.

LOCAL INTERACTION AND THE STAG HUNT

There is one modest general truth that is indisputable. That is that local interaction makes a difference. If we compare the two dynamics *best respond to your neighborhood* and *imitate the most successful strategy in your neighborhood* in a large population, with the whole population as your neighborhood, they have exactly the same basins of attraction. If more than one-third of the population are hare hunters, the dynamics takes the population to all hunting hare. If less than one-third of the population are hare hunters, then the stag hunters take over.

In the original large-population model with a small probability of mutation or experimentation, the underlying dynamics did not much matter. Whatever the underlying adaptive dynamics, the population spends most of its time hunting hare. When we move to local interaction this is no longer true. In local interaction, we have sensitivity to the underlying dynamics.[2]

That imitation and best-response dynamics can give different results in local interactions should really be no surprise, given the literature on local interactions in prisoner's dilemma. Many investigators have found that cooperators can survive in a spatial version of prisoner's dilemma. In some cases, the dynamics become very complex.[3] Under best-response dynamics there wouldn't be anything interesting to say. It is the defining feature of prisoner's dilemma that Defect is the best response to everything. Under best-response dynamics, the population would go immediately to a state where everyone defects. Local interaction models where cooperation persists in the prisoner's dilemma are all based on imitation or replication.

It would be a mistake to try to draw such sweeping conclusions as "local interaction favors hare hunting" or "local interaction favors stag hunting" in the stag hunt game. It would still be a mistake, although not quite as great a one, to say that local interaction with best response always leads to hare hunting, while local interaction with imitation always leads to stag hunting. But we can say that local interaction opens up possibilities of cooperation that do not exist in a more traditional setting, and that imitation dynamics is often more conducive to cooperation than best-response dynamics.[4]

OTHER INTERACTION STRUCTURES

The circle and the two-dimensional square lattice are the most thoroughly explored interaction structures, but they are certainly not the only ones worthy of consideration. Consider the following fable.[5] There is a central figure in the group who interacts (pairwise) with all others and with whom they interact – you might think of this figure as the Boatman in honor of Hume or the Huntsman in honor of Rousseau. Every round, players revise their strategies by choosing the best response to their partners' prior play, with the exception that the Huntsman revises his strategy much less often. We add a small chance of spontaneously changing strategy for each player. If everyone hunts stag and the Huntsman spontaneously switches to hunting hare, in two rounds probably everyone will hunt hare. But conversely, if everyone is hunting hare and the Huntsman spontaneously switches to hunting stag, in two rounds probably everyone will hunt stag. In the long run, the population spends approximately half its time hunting hare and half its time hunting stag. Here, best-response dynamics does not force the social contract to have negligible probability in the long run. The *structure* of local interaction makes a difference.[6]

POISONERS REVISITED

I began the discussion of location with the example of poisoner bacteria that could not invade in a well-stirred mixture, but could when interacting with neighbors on a plate of agar. The point then was that local interaction can make a difference not just in models but in real experimental situations. No game theory model was presented at that point, but the reader may by now have been struck by suspicious similarities to the stag hunt. Poison-producing *E. coli* have the same growth rate no matter whom they encounter. Peaceful *E. coli* have a higher growth rate than the poisoners if they encounter each other, but are killed if they encounter the poisoners. There seems to be some analogy between the poison-producing bacteria and hare hunters, and between peaceful bacteria and stag hunters.

There are a number of formal local-interaction models of this bacterial interaction in the biological literature,[7] none of which is exactly of the form of the models that I have discussed here. And the actual biology of the interaction is much richer than any of the models. But there is nothing to prevent us from consideration of a local-interaction model that is loosely inspired by the real phenomenon. Suppose that in one generation an individual, located on a two-dimensional lattice, is replaced by the type with highest average success in the neighborhood. Success is determined by stag hunt games played with each of the neighbors, with the payoffs 3 for poisoners, 0 for peaceful bacteria who encounter poisoners, and 4 for peaceful bacteria who encounter each other. How can poisoners (hare hunters) invade, given the results of this chapter?

The poison diffuses on the agar plate, so that it affects not only nearest neighbors but also others farther away. But only immediate neighbors determine who replaces an individual (or is imitated). Here again, we have two different neighborhoods involved, but the interaction neighborhood is bigger than the imitation neighborhood.

For example, suppose that the imitation neighborhood is Moore (8) and the interaction neighborhood is Moore (24). We focus on the frontier between poisoners, P, and peaceful (nice) bacteria, N, in Figure 3.6. The imitation neighborhood of the boldface nice individual is indicated by italics. The diffusion of the poison extends the interaction neighborhood to all individuals shown. Poisoners interact with their twenty-four neighbors to get a total payoff of $(3)(24) = 72$. Front-line nice guys, such as the one indicated by boldface, interact with ten poisoners for no payoff and with fourteen other nice guys

NNNPP
N**NN**PP
N**NN**PP
N**NN**PP
NNNPP

Figure 3.6. Poisoners vs. Nice Guys

for a payoff of $(14)(4) = 56$. Second-line nice guys interact with nineteen of their own for a payoff of 76, and fortunate third-line nice guys get a payoff of 96.

But third-line nice guys are not in the imitation neighborhood. It only includes those that have been damaged to some degree by the poison. In the imitation neighborhood, poisoners have the highest average success. Poisoners advance on the frontier. Poisoners will take over the population.

If, however, we reverse the neighborhoods so that poisoning acts on a short range and imitation is based on a long range, then the nice guys drive out the poisoners – or, to revert to our original language, stag hunting spreads throughout the population.

PART II

SIGNALS

B ACTERIA float around in the ambient fluid. It is a danger-
ous life, where many perils are encountered. If a bacterium
bumps into a surface, it grabs it and holds on with tiny ap-
pendages called pili, exchanging a drifting, random-encounter
environment for a two-dimensional local-interaction one. The
bacteria aggregate in microcolonies, perhaps moving by twitch-
ing the pili. When there are enough microcolonies in an area,
the bacteria change their behavior. They build an external
polysaccharide matrix of some complexity, within which they
live as a community, largely protected from bacteriocidal agents
in the surrounding environment.

Such biofilms are responsible for persistent middle-ear infections in children and for pneumonia in patients with cystic
fibrosis. They grow on catheters and artificial heart valves. They
form in your own mouth every night, as gram-positive cocci
labor to construct cities of dental plaque, only to have their
handiwork destroyed by the morning toothbrushing. The dis-
coverer of bacteria, Anton van Leeuwenhoek, found them in
his own dental plaque and reported the results to the Royal
Society of London in a letter of September 17, 1683.

Efforts of isolated bacteria toward constructing the polysaccharide matrix would have been to no avail. How do bacteria know when the community is large enough to initiate the

plaque-building behavior? The fortuitous timing of the change in behavior is achieved by a process known as *quorum signaling*.[1]

Quorum signaling was originally discovered in a less sinister setting. Certain squid have a light organ that they use to camouflage themselves when foraging on moonlit nights. Without some countermeasures, they would be visible as a dark patch to predators below them. The squid regulate the light output to render themselves effectively invisible. The light, however, is not produced by the squid itself. It is produced by symbiotic bacteria, *Vibrio fisheri,* that inhabit the light organ of the squid.[2]

These bacteria are found at low densities in the open ocean, and at low densities they do not emit light at all. But at high densities, when they sense a "quorum," they emit a blue-green light. Quorum sensing depends on a signaling molecule that the bacteria emit, which diffuses into the environment. High densities of the bacteria lead to high concentrations of the molecule, which activates genes that are responsible for the luminescence. During the day, or on a moonless night, the squid lowers the concentration of bacteria by expelling some into the ocean, thus turning off the lights. On a moonlit night, the squid allows the bacteria to rapidly multiply in its light organ to produce the desirable luminescence.

Quorum signaling in bacteria is by no means confined to the two instances just described. It seems quite widespread – playing a role in all kinds of cooperative bacterial enterprises. It is one of several signals used by the remarkable bacterium *Myxococcis xanthus*. When food conditions are scarce, the individual bacteria aggregate into mounds. They then differentiate into specialized cells. Some die to provide food for the others. Some form a stalk. Some become spores at the top of the stalk, are dispersed, and lie dormant until better times return.[3] Quorum signaling is used to sense when starvation is widespread. The formation of the multicellular fruiting body involves other signals as well. The biochemistry of a number of these signals has been studied,[4] although much remains to be explained before we have a complete analysis of fruiting body development. In times when food is adequate, these myxobacteria are free-living individuals in the soil, but as such their actions are not always independent. They engage in coordinated attacks on larger microbial prey and overwhelm them with secreted enzymes.[5] *Myxococcis xanthus* has solved the problem of the stag hunt.

4

EVOLUTION OF INFERENCE

PHILOSOPHICAL SKEPTICISM

JEAN-Jacques Rousseau begins his discussion of the origin of language in *A Discourse on Inequality* by toying with a paradox:

> [A] substitution of voice for gesture can only have been made by common consent, something rather difficult to put into effect by men whose crude organs had not yet been exercised; something indeed, even more difficult to conceive of having happened in the first place, for such a unanimous agreement would need to be proposed, which means that speech seems to be absolutely necessary to establish the use of speech.[1]

Rousseau moves on without taking the problem seriously, but the paradox echoes through modern philosophy of language. How can we explain the genesis of speech without presupposing speech, reference without presupposing reference, meaning without presupposing meaning? A version of this paradox forms the basis of Quine's attack on the logical empiricist doctrine that logic derives its warrant from conventions of meaning – that logical truths are true and logical inferences are valid by virtue of such conventions. Quine raised the general

This chapter is largely drawn from Skyrms (2000).

skeptical question of how conventions of language could be established without preexisting language, as well as calling attention to more specific skeptical circularities. If conventions of logic are set up by explicit definitions, or by axioms, must we not presuppose logic to unpack those conventions?

CONVENTION ACCORDING TO DAVID LEWIS

David Lewis (1969) sought to answer these skeptical doubts within a game theoretical framework in his book *Convention*. This account contains fundamental new insights, and I regard it as a major advance in the theory of meaning. Lewis sees a convention as being a special kind of strict Nash equilibrium in a game that models the relevant social interaction. To say that a convention is a Nash equilibrium is to say that if an individual deviates from a convention that others observe, he is no better off for that. To say that it is a *strict* Nash equilibrium is to say that he is actually worse off. To this, Lewis adds the additional requirement that an individual unilateral deviation makes *everyone* involved in the social interaction worse off, so that it is in the common interest to avoid such deviations.

A theory of convention must answer two fundamental questions: How do we arrive at conventions? And by virtue of what considerations do conventions remain in force? Within Lewis's game-theoretic setting, these questions become, respectively, the problems of *equilibrium selection* and *equilibrium maintenance*.

On the face of it, the second problem may seem to have a trivial solution – the equilibrium is maintained because it is an equilibrium! No one has an incentive to deviate. In fact, since it is a strict equilibrium, everyone has an incentive not to deviate. This is part of the answer, but Lewis shows that this is not the whole answer.

There is an incentive to avoid unilateral deviation, but, for example, if you expect me to deviate, you might believe you would be better off deviating as well. And if I believe that you have such beliefs, I may expect you to deviate and by virtue of such expectations deviate myself. It is when I believe that others will not deviate that I must judge deviation to be against my own interest. The self-reinforcing character of a strict Nash equilibrium must be backed by a hierarchy of appropriate interacting expectations.

These considerations lead to Lewis's introduction of the concept of *common knowledge*. A proposition, P, is common knowledge among a group of agents if each of them knows that P, and each of them knows that each of them knows that P, and so forth for all finite levels. To the requirement that a convention must be the appropriate kind of strict Nash equilibrium, he adds the additional requirement that it be backed by the appropriate kind of common knowledge. The game being played must be common knowledge to the players, along with the fact that their actions are jointly at the equilibrium of the game that constitutes the convention.

Considerations of common knowledge are thus at the center of Lewis's theory of equilibrium maintenance. What about equilibrium selection? A convention is typically an equilibrium in an interaction, which admits many different equilibria. That is what makes conventions conventional. An alternative equilibrium might have done as well. How, then, do the agents involved come to coordinate on one of the many possible equilibria involved? Lewis, following Thomas Schelling, identifies three factors that may affect equilibrium selection: prior agreement, precedent, and salience. A *salient* equilibrium (Schelling's focal equilibrium) is one that "stands out" to the agents involved for some reason or another. Salience is a psychological property, and the causes of salience are not restricted in any way. Prior agreement and precedent can be viewed as special sources of salience.

Lewis discusses the conventionality of meaning in the context of signaling games.[2] We suppose that one player, the Sender, comes into possession of some private knowledge about the world and wishes to share it with another player, the Receiver, who could use that knowledge to make a more informed decision. The decision has payoff implications for both Sender and Receiver, and their interests in this decision are common, which is why both wish the decision to be an informed one.

The Sender has a number of potential messages or signals that he can send to the Receiver to convey that information, the only hitch being that the "messages" have no preexisting meaning. The model that Lewis considers has an equal number of states of the world, S, messages, M, and acts, A. The payoffs for both players make the game a game of common interest. For example, where the number of states, messages, and acts is three, we might have payoffs

	Act I	Act 2	Act 3
State 1	1,1	0,0	0,0
State 2	0,0	1,1	0,0
State 3	0,0	0,0	1,1

(where payoffs are entered as sender payoff, receiver payoff). We will assume in this example that states are equiprobable.

A *Sender's strategy* in this game is a rule that associates each state with a message to be sent in that state; a *Receiver's strategy* associates each message with an act to be taken if the message has been received. Sender's strategy and Receiver's strategy taken together associate an act taken by the Receiver with each state of the world. If, for every state, the act taken is optimal for that state, the combination of Sender's strategy and Receiver's strategy is called a *signaling system*. For example, for three states, messages, and acts, the following is an example of a signaling system.

Sender's Strategy	Receiver's Strategy
$S_1 \rightarrow M_1$	$M_1 \rightarrow A_1$
$S_2 \rightarrow M_2$	$M_2 \rightarrow A_2$
$S_3 \rightarrow M_3$	$M_3 \rightarrow A_3$

It is evident, however, that this is not the only signaling system for this game. If we take it, and permute the messages in any way, we get another equally good signaling system, for example,

Sender's Strategy	Receiver's Strategy
$S_1 \rightarrow M_3$	$M_3 \rightarrow A_1$
$S_2 \rightarrow M_1$	$M_1 \rightarrow A_2$
$S_3 \rightarrow M_2$	$M_2 \rightarrow A_3$

Thus, the meaning of a message is a function of which signaling system is operative. Meaning emerges from social interaction.

Signaling systems are clearly Nash equilibria of the sender-receiver game. They are not the only Nash equilibria of the game. There are totally noncommunicative equilibria, where the Sender always sends the same message and the Receiver performs the same action regardless of the message received, such as

Sender's Strategy	Receiver's Strategy
$S_1 \rightarrow M_1$	$M_3 \rightarrow A_2$
$S_2 \rightarrow M_1$	$M_1 \rightarrow A_2$
$S_3 \rightarrow M_1$	$M_2 \rightarrow A_2$

This is an equilibrium, no matter how inefficient it is, since neither player can improve a payoff by unilaterally switching strategies. There are equilibria in which partial information is transmitted, such as

Sender's Strategy	Receiver's Strategy
$S1 \rightarrow M_1$	$M_1 \rightarrow A_1$
$S2 \rightarrow M_1$	$M_2 \rightarrow A_1$
$S3 \rightarrow M_3$	$M_3 \rightarrow A_3$

These games contain many equilibria, some of which are signaling systems and some of which are not.

But signaling systems are special. They are not only Nash equilibria but also strict Nash equilibria. (And they are the kind of strict Nash equilibria that are *conventions* in Lewis's general theory of convention.) The other non–signaling system equilibria do not come up to these standards. Unilaterally changing a potential response to an unsent message, or unilaterally changing the circumstance in which you send a message that will be ignored, is of no consequence. It does not make one better off, but it does not make one worse off either. So signaling systems are conventions, and the only conventions, in the kind of sender-receiver game that has been described.[3]

Lewis's account is a fundamental advance in the philosophy of meaning. It focuses attention on social interaction and information transmission. And it provides an account of how conventions of meaning can be maintained. Still, it does not appear that Lewis's account has completely answered the skeptical doubts with which we began.

Where did all the common knowledge come from? The skeptic is certainly entitled to ask for the origin of the common knowledge invoked by the account of equilibrium maintenance. And the skeptic can also ask for a noncircular account of equilibrium selection for equilibria that constitute conventions of meaning. Prior agreement and precedent can hardly be invoked to explain the genesis of meaningful signals. And where is the salience in Lewis's models of signaling games? All signaling system equilibria are equally good. None seems especially salient. Perhaps some sort of salience extrinsic to the model might get us off the ground, but we lack any explicit theory of such salience.

BACTERIA DO IT

Wait a minute! Before we let ourselves become too confused by philosophical skepticism, we should remember that bacteria have developed and maintain effective signaling systems. They do this without benefit of common knowledge, intentionality, or rational choice. Perhaps we have not been looking at the problem in the right way.

In fact, signaling systems are ubiquitous at all levels of biological organization.[4] The honeybee has a signaling system that successfully encodes and transmits information regarding the location and quality of a food source. Birds use signals for warning, indicating territory, and mating. The species-specific alarm calls of the vervet monkeys, which are the focus of D. Cheney and R. M. Seyfarth's delightful book *How Monkeys See the World*, give us a particularly nice example. Vervets are prey to three main kinds of predator: leopards, snakes, and eagles. For each there is a different alarm call, and each alarm call elicits a different action, appropriate to the type of predator that triggers the call. The situation is remarkably close to that modeled in a Lewis sender-receiver game. Other nonprimate species, such as meerkats and some birds, also instantiate a similar game structure in their alarm calls.

Let us see what happens if we approach Lewis signaling games from the point of view of the evolutionary process – presupposing nothing that could not in principle apply at the level of bacteria, or below. If we start in this way we do not cut ourselves off from the rest of the biological world, and the theory can be augmented as appropriate when applied to organisms with intelligence, knowledge, intentionality, or rationality.

EVOLUTION

J. Maynard Smith and G. Price (1973) introduced a notion of equilibrium maintenance into evolutionary theory, that of an *evolutionarily stable strategy*. The leading idea is that an evolutionarily stable strategy must be able to resist invasion by a small number of mutants. Applying this in a plain-vanilla, large-population, random-encounter evolutionary model, this yields the definition of Maynard Smith and G. Parker (1976) – in a population playing the strategy, either the natives do better against themselves than a mutant, or both do equally well against the natives, but the natives do better against the mutant.

Suppose we have a species in which an individual sometimes finds herself or himself in the role of Sender, sometimes in the role of Receiver. Individuals have "strategies" (or rules or routines) that determine how they play the game in each role. Suppose that a population consists of individuals who all have the same strategy, which is a signaling system in a Lewis signaling game. If you consider potential mutations to other strategies in the game, you will see that a signaling system is here an evolutionarily stable strategy.

If we look for evolutionarily stable strategies of the signaling game other than signaling systems, we find that they do not exist. The other Nash equilibria of the game correspond to strategies that fail the test of evolutionary stability. For example, consider a population with the noninformative strategy of always sending the same signal, regardless of the state observed, and always taking the same act, regardless of the signal received. That population can be invaded by a mutant playing a signaling system. When playing against natives, both types do equally badly. But when playing against mutants, mutants rather than natives do the best.[5] Evolutionary stability gives a qualitative account of equilibrium maintenance with no presuppositions of common knowledge or rationality.

But how do we get to a particular equilibrium in the first place? We find one attractive suggestion in a remarkable passage from Darwin's (1898) *Descent of Man:*

> Since monkeys certainly understand much that is said to them by man, and when wild, utter signal cries of danger to their fellows; and since fowls give distinct warnings for danger on the ground, or in the sky from hawks (both, as well as a third cry, intelligible to dogs), may not an unusually wise ape-like animal have imitated the growl of a beast of prey, and thus have told his fellow-monkeys the nature of the expected danger? This would have been the first step in the formation of language.[6]

Darwin knows of species-specific alarm calls. Modern studies support his remarks about the alarm calls of fowl.[7] He knows that one species may be able to use the information in another species' alarm call. Cheney and Seyfarth found that vervets use the information in the alarm calls of the Superb starling. Darwin also has a hypothesis about the genesis of animal signaling.

Darwin's hypothesis is that the crucial determinant of the signaling system selected is *natural salience*. The prey imitate the natural sounds of the predator to communicate the presence of the predator to their fellows. The only problem with this suggestion is that there seems to be no empirical evidence in support of it. For other kinds of animal signals, such as threat displays, natural salience provides a plausible explanation for the origin of the signal. Baring of teeth in dogs retains its natural salience. But species-specific alarm calls do not resemble the sounds made by the type of predator that they indicate. Of course, it is still possible that they began in the way suggested by Darwin, and that the course of evolution so modified them that their origins are no longer discernible. But in the absence of evidence to this effect, we are led to ask whether signaling systems could evolve without benefit of natural salience.

We can approach this question by applying a simple model of large-population, random-mixing differential reproduction, *replicator dynamics,*[8] to a Lewis sender-receiver game. We can let all kinds of combinations of Sender and Receiver strategies arise in the population, and run the replicator dynamics. Signaling systems *always* evolve. This can be shown both by computer simulation, and – in simple cases – analytically.[9]

The signaling system that evolves is not always the same. Each possible signaling system evolves for some initial population proportions. But the equilibria that are not signaling systems never evolve. The reason for this is that they are dynamically unstable. Only signaling systems are attractors in the evolutionary dynamics.

If natural salience had been present at the start of the process, it could have had the effect of constraining initial conditions so as to fall within the basin of attraction of a "natural signaling system." In the absence of natural salience, where meaning is purely conventional, signaling systems arise spontaneously, but which signaling system is selected depends on the vagaries of the initial stages of the evolutionary process.

Evolutionary dynamics has provided a remedy for our skepticism. We have an account of the spontaneous emergence of signaling systems that does not require preexisting common knowledge, agreement, precedent, or salience.

LEARNING

Is the point confined to strictly evolutionary settings? Adam Smith (1761), in *Considerations Concerning the First Formation of*

Languages, suggested a different approach:

> Two savages, who had never been taught to speak, but had been
> bred up remote from the societies of men, would naturally begin
> to form that language by which they would endeavor to make
> their mutual wants intelligible to each other, by uttering certain
> sounds, whenever they meant to denote certain objects.[10]

Smith is suggesting that, given the proper incentives, signaling systems can arise naturally from the dynamics of
learning.

It is not feasible to carry out Smith's thought experiment exactly, but A. Blume, D. V. deJong, Y.-G. Kim, and G. B. Sprinkle
(2001) saw whether undergraduates at the University of Iowa
would spontaneously learn to play some signaling system in
a Sender-Receiver game of the kind discussed by Lewis. They
take extraordinary precautions to exclude natural salience from
the experimental setting. Sender and Receiver communicate to
each other over a computer network. The messages available to
the Sender are the asterisk and the pound sign, {*,#}. These are
identified to the players as possible messages on their computer
screens. The order in which they appear on a given player's
screen is chosen at random to control for the possibility that
order of presentation might function as the operative salience
cue. Then players repeatedly play a Lewis signaling game. They
are kept informed of the history of play of the group. Under
these conditions, the players rapidly learn to coordinate on one
signaling system or another.

The result might be expected, because the qualitative dynamical behavior of the replicator dynamics that explain evolutionary emergence of signaling systems is shared by a wide
range of adaptive dynamics.[11] In Lewis signaling games, which
are games of common interest, evolutionary dynamics, learning dynamics, and almost any reasonable sort of adaptive dynamics lead to successful coordination on a signaling system

equilibrium. In the absence of natural salience, which signaling system emerges depends on the vicissitudes of initial conditions and chance aspects of the process. But some signaling system does evolve because signaling systems are powerful attractors in the dynamics, and other Nash equilibria of the game are dynamically unstable.

LOGIC?

The dynamics of evolution and learning show us how signaling systems can emerge spontaneously. The skeptical questions concerning equilibrium selection and equilibrium maintenance are completely answered by the dynamical approach. But we should remember that the thrust of Quine's skepticism was directed at conventionalist accounts of logic. And although our account of the dynamics of Lewis signaling games has given us an account of the emergence of a kind of meaning, it has not given us an account of logical truth or logical inference based on that meaning.

Pursuit of such a theory would have to take on some of the complexity of thought that I have deliberately excluded from the basic model. We are still very far from an account of the evolution of logic, and I do not have any general account to offer here. I would like only to indicate a few small steps that we can take in the desired direction.

PROTO-TRUTH FUNCTIONS

As a first step, I propose that we modify Lewis signaling games to allow for the possibility that the Sender's observation gives less than perfect information about the relevant state of the world. For example, suppose that a vervet Sender could sometimes determine the exact kind of predator, but sometimes tell only that it is a leopard or a snake.

It may well be that the optimal evasive action, given that a leopard or snake is present, is different from either the optimal act for leopard or the optimal act for snake. One would not want to stumble on the snake while running for the nearest tree to escape the leopard. One would not want to draw a leopard's attention by standing up straight and scanning the ground for snakes.[12] A new message should not be hard to come by. (In fact, vervets that have migrated to new localities where they are faced with new predators that call for new evasive action have developed new messages and the appropriate signaling system.)[13]

So we now have a model with four types of knowledge that Senders may have, four messages, and four states with a common interest payoff structure as before. Then, the evolutionary (or learning) dynamics is no different than the one we would have if we had four predators, four messages, and four appropriate evasive actions in the original setting. The story is the same. A signaling system will emerge with signals for eagle, snake, leopard, and *leopard or snake*. The last signal I call a *proto-truth function*. The truth function "or" is a sentence connective which forms a compound sentence that is true just in case at least one of its constituent simple sentences is true. The last signal need not be a complex sentence with meaningful parts, one of which is the truth function "or," but one way of giving its meaning is as such a truth function.[14]

More generally, we can modify the Lewis model by letting nature decide randomly the specificity with which the Sender can identify the state of nature.[15] Then, given the appropriate common interest structure, we have the conditions for the emergence of a rich signaling system with lots of proto-truth functional signals.

We are now well out of the vervets' league, and perhaps into the province of "an unusually wise ape-like animal," but I will continue to frame my example in terms of the vervets for the sake of narrational continuity. Our Sender may now have proto-truth functional signals for both "snake or leopard" and for "not-leopard."

INFERENCE

Now I would like to complicate the model a little more. Most of the time, one member of the troop detects a predator, gives the alarm call appropriate to his or her state of knowledge, and everything goes as in the last section. This predominant scenario is sufficiently frequent to fix a signaling system, which includes proto-truth functions.

Occasionally, two members of the troop detect a predator at the same time, and both give alarm calls. Sometimes they both have maximally specific information, and both give the alarm call for the specific predator. Sometimes, however, they will have complementary imprecise information as, for example, when one signals *snake or leopard* and the other signals *not-leopard*.

Since the Senders detect the presence of a predator independently and at approximately the same time, they just use their strategies in the signaling game of the last section. What do the Receivers do? Initially, some will do one thing and some will do another. Those who take the evasive action appropriate to snakes will, on average, fare better than those who don't. Over time, evolution, learning, or any reasonable adaptive dynamics will fix this behavior. Here we have a kind of evolution of inference, where the inference is based on the kind of meaning explicated by Lewis signaling games.

The setting need not be the Amboseli forest preserve, and the signaling game need not involve alarm calls. The essential points are that a signaling system evolves for communicating partial information, that the Receiver may get multiple signals encoding various pieces of information, and that it is in the common interest of Sender and Receiver that the latter takes the action that is optimal in light of all the information received. When these conditions are realized, adaptive dynamics favors the emergence of inference.

5

CHEAP TALK

IN sender-reciever situations where the transfer of information is in the interest of both parties, signals spontaneously acquire meaning and act to promote the common interest. But what about types of interaction that do not have this ideal structure? Some people may want to withhold information, or to transmit misinformation. Concealment and deception also are used by organisms other than humans. Every potential employee wants to convince employers that she is intelligent and hardworking. Every antelope would like to convince the wolf that she is too fast to catch. Nobel laureate in economics A. Michael Spence and later evolutionary biologist Amotz Zahavi[1] suggested that in such situations, we might find considerable resources expended on signals that are too costly to fake. A degree in classics from Harvard may represent acquisition of knowledge irrelevant to an occupation but still serve as a reliable signal of intelligence and enterprise. A conspicuous vertical leap by an antelope may serve as a reliable signal of speed and evasive capability. Zahavi's "Handicap Principle" makes cost the key element in the analyis of the evolution of signaling.[2] Given

This chapter is largely drawn from Skyrms (2002).

these developments, it is easy to be skeptical about the efficacy of costless signals in situations that lack the ideal structure of David Lewis's sender-receiver games. Talk is cheap.

PRISONER'S DILEMMA AND THE SECRET HANDSHAKE

What kind of interaction could support more skepticism about the efficacy of cost-free preplay communication than the prisoner's dilemma? A self-interested agent is better off defecting, no matter what the other player does. How, then, could any preplay communication of intention make any difference to the players' decisions?[3]

Arthur Robson, in an article subtitled "Darwin, Nash and the Secret Handshake" (1990), was the first to point out that cheap talk (costless preplay communication) may have an important effect in evolutionary games. He considered a population composed of individuals defecting in the prisoner's dilemma. If there is a signal not used by this population, a mutant could invade by using this signal as a "secret handshake." Mutants would defect against the natives and cooperate with each other. They would then do better than natives and would be able to invade. Without cheap talk, a population of defectors in prisoner's dilemma would be evolutionarily stable. With cheap talk this is no longer true.

This is not to say that cheap talk establishes cooperation in the prisoner's dilemma. Mutants who fake the secret handshake and then defect can invade a population of the previous kind of mutants. And then if there is still an unused message, it can be used by a third round of mutants as a secret handshake. It seems that the whole story may be fairly complex. The point is not that a cooperative equilibrium has been created, but that a noncooperative equilibrium has been destabilized.

How strong is this conclusion? Granted that if all natives defect and there is an unused signal, cooperators can invade using a secret handshake. But what if we have a population state where all natives defect, but some send one signal and some send another, with all signals being used by some substantial portion of the population? Then the secret handshake won't work and cooperators can't invade.

Nevertheless, such a population is not quite in an evolutionarily stable state. It is in what is called a neutrally stable state: Mutants can't do better than the natives, but they might not do worse. In such an environment, one signal sent is as good as another. Whatever signals are sent, everyone defects. For this reason, the proportions of the population sending different signals could be perturbed without there being any restoring selection force. If the population were eventually to drift into a state where some signal was not used, the door would open for cooperators using a secret handshake.

On the other hand, a state where everyone cooperates cannot be even neutrally stable, because mutants who send a cooperator's signal and then defect do better than the natives and invade the population. So I reiterate, the effect of the signals here is not to create a stable cooperative equilibrium, but rather to destabilize a noncooperative one. Still, this is something that should not be neglected.

STAG HUNT AND THE HANDICAP PRINCIPLE

In a note provocatively titled "Nash Equilibria Are not Self-Enforcing," Robert Aumann (1990) argues that cheap talk cannot be effective in the following game:

Aumann's Stag Hunt

	c	d
Stag c	9,9	0,8
Hare d	8,0	7,7

In this base game, there are two pure-strategy Nash equilibria, *cc* and *dd*. The first is Pareto-dominant and the second is safer (risk-dominant).

Aumann points out that no matter which act a player intends to do, he has an interest in leading the other player to believe that he will do *c*. If the other so believes, she will do *c*, which yields the first player a greater payoff. One can think of *c* as hunting stag and *d* as hunting hare, where diverting the other player to hunting stag increases a hare hunter's chances of getting the hare. Then both stag hunting types and hare hunting types will wish the other player to believe that they are stag hunters. Aumann concludes that all types of players will send the message "I am a stag hunter," and consequently that these messages convey no information.[4]

Evidently, the argument applies equally well to all those stag hunt games that are sometimes called assurance games, which are, by definition, those in which hare hunting against a stag hunter is better than hare hunting against a hare hunter. These are all games in which Zahavi's Handicap Principle comes into play. Since hare hunters stand to profit by communicating misinformation, we should only see communication in equilibrium if hare hunters must pay an appropriate cost. If there is no cost, then informative signaling should not evolve.

Following the publication of Aumann's argument, two experimental studies explicitly testing the hypothesis that cheap talk would not be effective in assurance games were added to a rather substantial experimental corpus on effectiveness of cheap talk.[5] Gary Charness (2000) and Kenneth Clark, Stephen Kay, and Martin Sefton (2000) both find that with costless preplay communication in an Aumann-type assurance game, the frequency of a successful stag Hunt goes up. (It does not go up quite as dramatically as in stag hunt games where there is no motive to send a misleading signal, but it goes up substantially.)

These results should, at least, occasion a little more thought about cost-free preplay communication in assurance games.

Let us examine the issue a little more closely by embedding a stag hunt of the assurance type in an evolutionary game with cheap talk. For maximum simplicity, we will use only two signals. Interaction now has two parts. First, players exchange signals. Next, they play the stag hunt, with the possibility of conditioning their move on the signal received from the other player. A player's strategy in this cheap-talk game specifies *which signal to send, what act to do if signal 1 is received,* and *what act to do if signal 2 is received.* There are eight strategies in this game. We want to investigate the evolutionary dynamics of stag hunt with cheap talk.

What is the equilibrium structure? First, we must notice that some states where everyone hunts hare are unstable equilibria. For instance, if the entire population has the strategy "Send signal 1 and hunt hare no matter what signal you receive," then a mutant could invade using the unused signal as a secret handshake. That is, the mutant strategy "Send signal 2 and hunt stag if you receive signal 2, but if you receive signal 1 hunt hare" would hunt hare with the natives and hunt stag with its own kind, and would thus do strictly better than the natives. The replicator dynamics would carry the mutants to fixation.

Next, neither a population of hare hunters that sends both messages nor any population composed exclusively of stag hunters is in an evolutionarily stable state. The proportions of those who hunt hare and send message 1 to those who hunt hare and send message 2 could change with no payoff penalty. Likewise with the case where all hunt stag. These states are neutrally stable, rather than evolutionarily stable.

There is, however, an evolutionarily stable state in the cheap-talk game. It is *an entirely new equilibrium, which has been created by the signals!* This is a state of the population in which half the population has each of the strategies.

<1, hare, stag>
<2, stag, hare>

The first strategy sends signal 1, hunts hare if it receives signal 1, and hunts stag if it receives signal 2. The second sends signal 2, hunts stag if it receives signal 1, and hunts hare if it receives signal 2. These strategies cooperate with each other, but not with themselves! Notice that in a population that has only these two strategies, the replicator dynamics must drive them to the $\frac{50}{50}$ equilibrium.[6] If there are more who play the first strategy, the second gets a greater average payoff; if there are more of the second, the first get a greater average payoff.[7] One can check that this state is evolutionarily stable. Any mutant would do strictly worse than the natives and would be driven to extinction by the replicator dynamics. It is also true that this is the *only* evolutionarily stable state in this game.[8]

Here, cost-free communication has not only destabilized old equilibria but also created an entirely new, evolutionarily stable equilibrium. Furthermore, notwithstanding Aumann's argument, and in violation of at least some readings of the Handicap Principle, in this equilibrium *the signals carry perfect information about the response type of the Sender*. And that information is utilized by the Receiver, in that he performs an act that is a best response to the Sender's response to the signal he himself has sent.

BARGAINING AND BASINS OF ATTRACTION

Let us return to the Nash bargaining game of Chapter 2. Each player makes a demand for a fraction of the pie. If their demands total more than 1, no bargain is struck and they get nothing. Otherwise, they get what they demand. We will focus on the simplest, discrete version of this game. In this simplified game, there are only three possible demands: $\frac{1}{3}$, $\frac{2}{3}$, and $\frac{1}{2}$, which we denote by acts 1, 2, and 3, respectively. The resulting evolutionary game has a unique evolutionarily stable strategy, demand-$\frac{1}{2}$, but it also has an evolutionarily stable polymorphic state in which half of the population demands $\frac{1}{3}$ and half of the population demands $\frac{2}{3}$. The polymorphic equilibrium squanders resources. Each strategy has an average payoff of $\frac{1}{3}$. The state where all demand $\frac{1}{2}$, and get it, is efficient.

Nevertheless, if we compute the basin of attraction in the replicator dynamics of demand-$\frac{1}{2}$ – the set of initial population proportions that the evolutionary dynamics carries to a state where everyone demands $\frac{1}{2}$ – it is only about 62 percent of the possible population proportions.[9] The wasteful polymorphism has a basin of attraction of 38 percent. (Another polymorphic equilibrium, in which demand-one-third has probability $\frac{1}{2}$, demand-half has probability $\frac{1}{6}$, and demand-two-thirds has probability $\frac{1}{3}$, is dynamically unstable and is never seen in simulations.)

What happens if we embed this game in a signaling game with three cost-free signals? A strategy in this cheap-talk game consists of the answers to four questions:

1. What signal should I send?
2. What demand should I make if I receive signal 1?
3. What demand should I make if I receive signal 2?
4. What demand should I make if I receive signal 3?

Each of these questions has three possible answers. There are now eighty-one strategies.

In the space of possible population proportions of these eighty-one strategies, how large is the basin of attraction of those final states where all demand $\frac{1}{2}$? Is it still about 62 percent? How large is the basin of attraction of those final states

where half the population demands $\frac{1}{3}$ and half demands $\frac{2}{3}$?
Is it still about 38 percent? Existing theory does not answer
these questions, but we can investigate them by Monte Carlo
simulation – sampling from the uniform distribution on the
81-simplex of population proportions, letting the population
evolve for a long enough time, repeating the process, and
collecting statistics.

When we do this,[10] more than 98 percent of the trials end
up with everyone demanding half. Counterparts of the old
$\frac{1}{3}$–$\frac{2}{3}$ polymorphism are not seen at all. (The remaining 1 to
2 percent of the trials lead to new polymorphic equilibria created by the signals.)[11] By looking not just at equilibrium but
also at dynamical behavior, we have found an important new
effect of costless signals. The exchange of signals has created a
dramatic increase in the size of the basin of attraction of the
equal split.

If we return to the stag hunts of the last section, we also find
significant shifts in the basins of attraction, but the picture is
different. Consider the assurance game with payoffs:

Stag against stag $= 1.00$
Stag against hare $= 0.00$
Hare against hare $= \ \ .60$
Hare against stag $= \ \ .61$

In the game without communication, hare hunting has the
largest basin of attraction. If up to 60.6 percent of the population hunts stag, the replicator dynamics still carries the population to a state where all hunt hare. When we add cost-free
communication with two signals, the results of a Monte Carlo
simulation[12] are

All hunt stag $59\frac{1}{2}\%$
All hunt hare 29%
Polymorphism $11\frac{1}{2}\%$

Signaling has shifted the largest basin of attraction (of about 60 percent) from hare hunting to stag hunting. The new polymorphism that signaling has created in the stag hunt also has a basin of attraction that is far from negligible.

In the bargaining game, the major action was not with the number of new polymorphic equilibria created but with the great expansion of the basin of attraction of equal division. How does the introduction of signals cause this change? Signals have no preexisting meaning. Does meaning evolve?

Consider the final states of trials in which the population ends up in a state where everyone demands $\frac{1}{2}$. In one trial, the population ended up with every type sending message 2 and every type demanding $\frac{1}{2}$ if they got message 2. But regarding what would be demanded if messages 1 or 3 were received, *every* possibility was represented in the population. In another example, messages 1, 2, and 3 were all sent in the population, but each strategy ignored the messages sent and simply demanded $\frac{1}{2}$ no matter which message was received. In between these two extremes there were all sorts of intermediate cases.

It is clear that in our setting, we do not have anything like the spontaneous generation of meaning that we see in Lewis sender-receiver games. The action of signals here is more subtle. Suppose we shift our attention from the strong notion of meaning that we get from a signaling system equilibrium in a sender-receiver game to the weaker notion of *information*. A signal carries information about a player if the probability that the player is in a certain category, given that he sent the signal, is different from the probability that he is in the category simply given that he is in the population. At equilibria where players all demand half, signals cannot carry information about the player's acts. Conceivably, signals could carry some information about a player's response type at equilibrium. But in the trials described in the previous paragraph this cannot be true, because in the first there is only one signal sent and in the second there is only one response type.

Perhaps the place to look for information in the signals is not at the end of the process but at the beginning and middle of evolution. For the signals to carry no information about response types at a randomly chosen initial state would take a kind of miracle. In almost all states, there is some information (in this probabilistic sense of information) about response types in the signals. There is information present – so to speak, by accident – at the beginning of evolution in our simulations. Any information about a response type could be exploited by the right kind of strategy. And the right kind of strategy is present in the population because all types are present. Strategies that exploit information present in signals will grow faster than other types. Thus, there will be an interplay between "accidental" information and the replicator dynamics.

We can investigate this interaction by computing at different times the average amount of information[13] in the messages in a population and averaging the results over many trials. The results of averaging over 1,000 trials are shown in Figure 5.1.

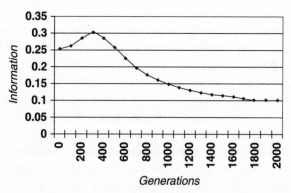

Figure 5.1. Evolution of Information

74

There is some information present at the onset of the trials "by accident." Then the replicator dynamics leads to an increase in average information in the signals, which peaks at about three hundred generations. After that, the average information in a signal begins a slow, steady decline.[14] What is the effect of this information? If there is information present in the population, there are strategies present that can use it to good effect. Thus, if we look only at the behaviors in the base bargaining game – as if cheap talk was invisible – we would expect to see some departure from random pairing. That is to say, the signals should induce some correlation in the behaviors in the bargaining game. The evolution of some correlations, averaged over 1,000 trials, is shown in Figure 5.2. The interaction between the information in the signals and the evolutionary dynamics generates a positive correlation between the compatible demands

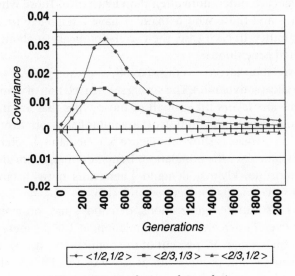

Figure 5.2. Evolution of Correlation

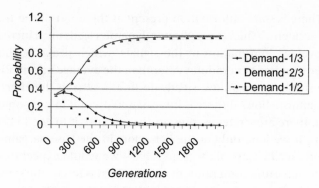

Figure 5.3. Evolution of Bargaining Behaviors

$(\frac{1}{2}, \frac{1}{2})$ and $(\frac{2}{3}, \frac{1}{3})$. Those who demand $\frac{1}{2}$ meet themselves more often than would be expected by chance. Those who demand $\frac{2}{3}$ and those who demand $\frac{1}{3}$ have a somewhat weaker tendency to meet each other more often than by chance. Those who demand $\frac{1}{2}$ and those who demand $\frac{2}{3}$ have a tendency to avoid one another. In each case, the correlation peaks at about four hundred generations.

Correlation affects average payoff, and thus growth under the replicator dynamics. The strong self-correlation of demand-$\frac{1}{2}$ behaviors favors the growth of those types that are implementing them. The evolution of bargaining behaviors, averaged over 1,000 trials, is shown in Figure 5.3. Demand-$\frac{1}{2}$ behaviors rapidly take over the population. Demand-$\frac{2}{3}$ behaviors die out even more quickly than demand-$\frac{1}{3}$ behaviors, notwithstanding the positive correlation between the two.

At four hundred generations, demand-$\frac{1}{2}$ has, on average, taken over 73 percent of the population; at 1,000 generations it has, on average, 97 percent of the population. At two thousand generations, positive and negative correlation has all but vanished, demand-$\frac{1}{2}$ behaviors have taken over 99 percent of the population, and little information remains in the signals.

What is the cause of the dramatic difference in the magnitude basins of attraction of the equal split produced by cheap talk (between 62 percent and 98+ percent)? It appears to be due to *transient* information. By way of a complex interaction of signaling strategies, this transient information produces transient covariation between behaviors in the base bargaining game. The net effect is to increment the fitness of strategies that demand $\frac{1}{2}$. When we get to equilibrium the information is gone, but it played a major role in selecting the equilibrium to be reached.

ANTICORRELATION

In the bargaining game, a positive correlation of demand-$\frac{1}{2}$ behaviors is important in achieving an efficient equilibrium where all demand $\frac{1}{2}$. But there are many interactions where a desirable equilibrium can only be achieved when behaviors are anticorrelated: You pull, I push; I cook, you set the table; you fish and I will row. Interactions that involve division of labor pose problems whose successful resolution requires anticorrelation. As the simplest model that exemplifies this problem, consider a game where players have the choice of two actions. If they both do the same thing they get 0 payoff, but if they do different things they get a payoff of 1. What is the effect of costless signaling in these situations?

First, let us consider the situation without signals. Suppose that there is a single population, large in size with random encounters. There are two types: act 1 and act 2. Standard evolutionary dynamics leads to a rather unsatisfactory equilibrium where the population is divided $\frac{50}{50}$ between these types. Suppose that act 1 types predominate. Then the rare act 2 types will usually encounter act 1 types and get a payoff of 1. Act 1 types will usually encounter each other and get a 0 payoff. The rare act 2 types will proliferate. In the same way, if act 2 types predominate, differential reproduction will favor act 1 types and drive the population toward the $\frac{50}{50}$ state. That state is not efficient because half the encounters are same-type encounters for a 0 payoff. The average payoff for the population is just $\frac{1}{2}$ – while the theoretic optimum with perfect anticorrelation would yield an average payoff of 1.

We embed this game in a cheap-talk game by adding two costless signals. There are now eight strategies, which answer

> Which signal do I send?
> What act if I get signal 1?
> What act if I get signal 2?

If we run a simulation, starting at randomly picked population proportions, the population *always* converges to a polymorphism that achieves an average payoff of $\frac{3}{4}$. This lies halfway between the payoff of $\frac{1}{2}$, achieved without signaling, and the utopia payoff of 1 that is possible with perfect division of labor. The $\frac{50}{50}$ equilibrium of the original game is still a theoretical possibility, but it is never seen. Signaling has rendered it dynamically unstable. All the action is at the new equilibria that have been created by signaling.

What are they like? Both signals are sent half the time. When an individual sending signal 1 meets an individual sending signal 2, they play different actions and get the optimal payoff. But when an individual meets another that sends the same signal, half the time it is an individual who does act 1 and half the time it is an individual who does act 2. This is true for each signal, and so the equilibrium state consists of a population of four strategies – each with equal proportions of the population.[15] Half the time, individuals meet those who send a different signal and get a payoff of 1. Half the time, individuals meet someone who sends the same signal, for an average payoff of $\frac{1}{2}$. Thus, we have the overall average payoff of $\frac{3}{4}$.

The foregoing describes the effect of two costless messages in the division-of-labor game within one[16] population. But division of labor may also be exemplified in interactions between two populations, as in mutualistic associations between species. Suppose individuals are drawn at random from each of two populations for the division-of-labor game. There is no longer a problem of meeting one's own kind. Perhaps cheap talk can attain greater payoff than $\frac{3}{4}$ when implemented between populations.

It can, but we don't really need the signals to achieve efficiency here. When the game without signals is played between two populations, evolutionary dynamics "always" achieves a division of labor, and a socially optimal average payoff of 1. (There is an equilibrium population state that is less than optimal, but it is dynamically unstable and is never seen in simulations.)

This can help us understand the one-population division of labor *with* signals. An agent who sends signal 1 can be thought of as engaged in two games: a game with others who send signal 1 and a game with those who send signal 2.[17] The first can be thought of as a one-population game within the subpopulation of signal 1 senders. The one-population evolutionary dynamics drives this subpopulation to a state where half do act 1 if they get signal 1 and half do act 2 if they get signal 1, for an average payoff of $\frac{1}{2}$. Likewise with the subpopulation that sends signal 2. These subpopulations can be thought of as in a two-population game with each other, with the operative strategic choice being what to do if you meet someone who sends a different signal. The two-population dynamics assures perfect anticorrelation on this question, giving us perfect efficiency in these encounters. This adds up to the signaling equilibria with average payoff of $\frac{3}{4}$ that we discussed in this section.

The foregoing analysis also tells us that in a one-population division-of-labor game with cheap talk, the more signals the better. More signals partition the population into more sub-populations, which can then effectively anticorrelate with each other.

COSTS AND THE PRISONER'S DILEMMA

Cheap talk has such powerful and unexpected consequences in the situations just examined that we might suspect that there could be a nice surprise when it is applied to the prisoner's dilemma. Suppose we embed the prisoner's dilemma in a game with two costless signals, just as we did with the stag hunt. What do we find if we repeatedly run the Monte Carlo simulation, choosing a starting population at random and letting the replicator dynamics run until it approaches an equilibrium?

We find that Defect always takes over the population. There are no miracles here. The secret handshake is no good if it isn't a secret, and it isn't a secret in a population where all strategies are represented. The type that gives the handshake and defects, no matter what, does better than the type that gives the handshake and cooperates with others just in case they give it too.

What if we make one signal costly and the other free? Can cooperators use the costly signal as a "handicap handshake" to stabilize a cooperative equilibrium? It doesn't do any good. Unconditional defectors who pay the same price to send the costly signal do better than the cooperators who send it.

What we need to stabilize cooperation are signals with differential costs for different response types. Suppose that signal 1 is free to those who cooperate just in case they get signal 1, but very costly to all other response types. And suppose that signal 2 is free to all. Then a population composed of those who send signal 1, cooperate with those who send signal 1, and defect against those who send signal 2 may be a stable equilibrium. Other mutant types who send signal 1 would be eliminated by the high costs, and those who send signal 2 would suffer defection from the natives while the natives benefited from cooperation among themselves. The example is somewhat contrary to the spirit of Zahavi in that the native "honest signalers" of conditional cooperation pay no signaling costs at all.

These differential costs may or may not strike you as stuffing the rabbit into the hat. In any case, they have taken us quite far from both our original topic of cost-free communication and the payoff structure of the prisoner's dilemma.

CHEAP TALK EVALUATED

No-cost, or low-cost, communication occurs all the time. We have seen how in the simplest large-population, random-encounter, replicator dynamics, evolutionary setting, this communication can have major effects on the evolutionary process. Cost-free communication can destabilize equilibria in the ensuing game. It can create new polymorphic equilibria that could not exist without communication. It can radically alter the size of basins of attraction of behaviors in the base game – for instance, tipping the balance from All Hunt Hare to All Hunt Stag in the stag hunt game. It is a mistake to omit cost-free communication from the analysis because "talk is cheap."

PART III

ASSOCIATION

THE bacterium *Myxococcus xanthus*, which accomplishes so much with a few signals, moves by gliding on slime trails. The exact mechanism of this action is unknown. But it is clear that using and following an existing slime trail is easier than laying one down from scratch, and the more that bacteria follow a trail, the more slime is laid down. It is observed that a bacterium approaching an existing slime trail at an angle will change direction to follow the trail. If the trail is not used, it dries up. Ants and tropical termites, and even some bees, use odor trails to guide their fellows to food sources.[1] Trails that are used successfully to find food are reinforced on the return trip. If a trail is not used, the pheromones quickly evaporate and the trail vanishes. The mechanism is of such value that it has evolved independently by different routes: from "tandem running" in ants and from an "alarm trail" to a damaged portion of the nest in termites.[2]

These organisms have evolved a remarkable implementation of reinforcement learning. The qualitative foundations of reinforcement learning were laid by the American psychologist William L. Thorndike at the beginning of the twentieth century. He was an undergraduate English major, but he changed direction upon reading William James's *Principles of Psychology*. Thorndike then went to Harvard to study with James, and

James even let Thorndike raise chickens for animal learning experiments in the basement of his house. Thorndike thought that a number of basic principles apply to both human and animal learning, and he thought of these processes as involving changes in the strength of neural connections. In ants and termites, the reinforcement learning is not implemented neurally, but rather by an external communally shared trail. Consider an ant trail to a food source. So long as the source is good, returning ants make the pheromone concentration along the trail stronger, thus implementing Thorndike's *Law of Effect:* An action that leads to positive rewards becomes more probable. If the food source is exhausted, the returning ants do not deposit pheromones along the trail, and the trail gradually evaporates, in accord with Thorndike's *Law of Practice:* An action that is not successfully used tends to become less probable.[3]

The slime trails of *Myxococcus xanthus* change in a slightly different way. In the absence of neither positive nor negative reward, the trails are enhanced by sheer frequency of use (which was how Thorndike originally thought all reinforcement learning in humans and animals worked).[4] In this respect, it has a connection with the mathematical theory of reinforced random walks. A random walk can be thought of as a model of random search behavior on some structure. For a simple example, take the structure to be the integers. An individual starts at zero, and then flips a coin to see whether the next move is up or down, and continues in this manner. The probabilities do not change. Persi Diaconis introduced the idea of a *reinforced* random walk in 1988. For each integer, there is a weight for the edge leading to the next highest number and a weight for the edge leading to the next lowest number. Initially all the weights are equal. An individual starts at zero and moves up or down with probability proportional to the weights of the *up* and *down* edges. But every time an edge is crossed, its weight is increased by one. Other reinforcement schemes have also been investigated.[5] The theory of reinforced random walks has been used to analyze the effect of slime trail reinforcement on aggregation behavior in *Myxococcus xanthus.*[6]

Reinforcement learning may well have something to teach us about the dynamics of association. Reinforcements might not be uniform but, rather, depend on the structure of interactions and the behavior of the individuals during the interactions. In this way, the static interaction structures of Part I may be generalized to dynamic interaction structures. Dynamics of interaction may be a crucial factor in the evolution of collective action.

6

CHOOSING PARTNERS

MAKING FRIENDS I

TEN strangers find themselves in a new location. Each morning, everyone wakes up and chooses someone to visit. Initially the process is random, but the visits result in interactions, and a pleasant interaction with someone makes it more likely the visitor will visit that person next time. Here is a simple model of the reinforcement dynamics. Each person has a numerical weight for each other person, and visits a person with probability proportional to his or her weight for that person. If, initially, all weights are equal, the process is random and visiting probabilities are equal. During a visit an interaction takes place, giving the visitor and host a payoff. At the end of the day, visitors and hosts update their weights for each other by adding their respective payoffs from their interaction to their old weights. The next day the process continues with the updated visiting probabilities.

All kinds of interesting interactions are possible, with all kinds of interesting outcomes. But we will start by looking at a very uninteresting interaction. Each visitor has an equally

---

For a more detailed treatment of the models discussed in this chapter and the next, see Skyrms and Pemantle (2000) and Pemantle and Skyrms (forthcoming a,b).

pleasant interaction, which we represent as a payoff of 1. The accommodating hosts have a payoff of 0 so that only the visitors are reinforced. We will suppose that everyone has an initial weight of 1 for everyone else, so that visiting starts out quite at random.

What sort of results can we expect from such a boring kind of uniform reinforcement? If we run a simulation of the process, we find a probabilistic interaction structure emerging. A given individual visits some individuals quite often and others hardly at all. Let the process run and these interaction probabilities settle down quickly[1] and eventually remain constant (to many decimal places). If we run the process again from the same starting point – equal initial weights and equal payoffs from any visit – we get convergence to a different set of interaction probabilities. The process can be repeated from the same starting points, and the emergence of all sorts of novel interaction structures will be observed. Some readers may find these simulation results very counterintuitive, but they are not the result of programming error. They are what should be expected according to theoretical analysis. But before I make good that claim, try to put yourself in the position of a sociologist or anthropologist who observed the behavior of these individuals. (The payoffs and the dynamical rule are not observable.) Imagine what blind alleys you might be led into, in your attempts to explain the emergent structure.

The scenic route to the analysis involves a little historical digression. Notice that the reinforcement dynamics is equivalent to each player's having an urn with one ball of each of nine colors in it. A player draws a ball and returns it with another ball of the same color (the reinforcement). This step is repeated. The process that I have just described is called a Pólya urn process after George Pólya, who introduced it as a model of contagion. Pólya's urn process is equivalent to the process generated in a rather different setting by a model of inductive inference.

Suppose that someone is considering rolls of a nine-sided die, which may be biased in any possible way. Suppose the person does not know the bias, and initially considers all possible biases to be equiprobable.[2] The person intends to roll the die and then update the degrees of belief on the evidence, roll again, and so forth. The sequence of degrees-of-belief in the outcome of the next trial forms the Bayes-Laplace process. Initially everything is equiprobable. If a ball of a given color is drawn, it becomes more probable that it will be drawn the next time. The probability of convergence is one, but convergence could be to *any* probabilities. And any probability is equally likely to be the one to which the process converges.

The Bayes-Laplace process and the Pólya urn process are mathematically equivalent. To make a long story short, our making-friends process will almost surely converge, but it can converge to *any* set of visiting probabilities.[3] A priori, for each player probabilities are uniform over all possible outcomes, with the players being independent. The moral of this simple model is not new, but it is worth restating in this context. Order can spontaneously emerge from a perfectly uniform starting point, with no sufficient reason to explain why it, rather than something else, should have emerged.

MAKING FRIENDS II

In the foregoing story only the visitor was reinforced. What if both the visitor and host are reinforced? We'll call this the friends II interaction, and in line with investigating what can emerge from a uniform situation, we will assume that on each visit both visitor and host are reinforced equally. If Bill visits Mary, Bill adds one to his weight for Mary and Mary adds one to her weight for Bill. As before, weights are updated at the end of each day, but we no longer have the simple Pólya urn dynamics. Reinforcement is *interactive*. Your weight changes depend not only on who you choose to visit, but also on who chooses to visit you. If we think of weights in terms of the urn metaphor, your urn is contaminated by others putting balls of their color in your urn. The analysis is not so simple as before.

If we run simulations of this process, we again see all kinds of structure emerging, but a general characterization of that structure is far from evident. Let us focus on the simplest case, where there are only three individuals. Sometimes we see a *symmetrical* structure emerging where one individual visits each of the other two half of the time. We can visualize this as a triangle with the individuals at the vertices and the edges representing visiting paths.

But sometimes we seem to see the emergence of an asymmetrical *"odd edge out"* structure where two of the individuals do not visit each other at all but always visit the third, and the third – the central character – splits his time between visiting the first and second.[4] This kind of structure is called a star.

The behavior of the friends II process was analyzed by Robin Pemantle.[5] The process converges and the limiting probabilities are always symmetric. I visit you with the same probability that you visit me. The stars are phantom stars; they disappear in the limit. Their existence in simulations just shows that the process has not run long enough to approach the limiting probabilities. But we find stars in a substantial number of simulations run for as long as five million iterations! Theory also confirms that this should happen.[6] If the vicissitudes of chance in the early stages of the process take it near one of the phantom star pseudoequilibria, it can take a very long time to escape and converge to a symmetric state.

The moral of the story depends on your perspective. From the standpoint of asymptotic theory, we have a very simple example where extensive computer simulations are a bad guide to limiting behavior. From the standpoint of social science, we have a process whose limiting behavior neglects possibilities that might be seen and appear stable in observations of large numbers of trials. In friends II, unlike friends I, convergence is slow, and long-lived transient behavior is an important part of the story.

MAKING ENEMIES

As before, ten strangers find themselves in a new location. Each morning, everyone wakes up and chooses someone to go visit. But now the visits are uniformly unpleasant. An unpleasant interaction with someone makes it less likely that the visitor will visit that person next time. We have two kinds of unpleasant visits: enemies I, where the visits are unpleasant to the visitor and neutral to the host, and enemies II, where the visits are unpleasant to both.

As a simple model, we can keep track of these negative payoffs by keeping a tally of *resistance weights*. The probability of visiting someone here will be the reciprocal of the resistance. There will be some nonzero initial resistance weights for every visit. They could all be equal for initial equal likelihood of visiting anyone. They could be unequal if for some reason it was more likely initially to visit one rather than another.

If we start with resistance weights equal or unequal, and if we consider making enemies I or making enemies II, the results are all the same. Each person is driven to equal probabilities of visiting each other person. Unlike friends II, convergence is rapid and computer simulation is in close agreement with limiting theory.[7] Positive reinforcement led to the spontaneous emergence of interaction structure. Negative reinforcement wipes out interaction structure, and leads to uniform random encounters.[8] It seems that the usual assumption of random encounters is more suitable for making enemies than for making friends.

POSITIVE AND NEGATIVE

Making friends and making enemies are both models where every choice leads to the same payoff. In conventional rational choice–based theory, there should be no difference between the two cases, because the standard theory of utility makes the choice of a zero point arbitrary. Ordinary experience and psychological theory disagree. D. Kahneman and A. Tversky (1979) and R. D. Luce (2000) develop more psychologically realistic choice models in which the zero point matters. Learning theories from W. K. Estes (1950) and R. R. Bush and F. Mosteller (1951), to the present day,[9] distinguish between positive and negative reinforcement. A recent experiment by Ido Erev, Yoella Bereby-Meyer, and Alvin Roth (1999) was designed specifically to look at the effect on learning dynamics of adding a constant to the payoffs so as to shift negative payoffs to positive ones. A clear difference was found.

The boundary between the payoffs producing positive reinforcement and negative reinforcement is sometimes called an *aspiration level* or a *satisficing level*. In some studies it is held fixed, but in more realistic theories it is allowed to adapt to past experience. If times are good, aspiration levels tend to rise; in hard times aspirations become more modest. There is, then, the question of the proper adaptive dynamics for aspiration levels. There is also the question of how positive and negative reinforcements are to be combined when both are present, in order to drive an adaptive dynamics for choices. There is a whole spectrum of learning models that arises from how one answers these questions. Different models may be appropriate for different applications. The general principle that uniform negative reinforcement tends to drive our visits in the direction of uniform random encounters holds good across a broad range of these theories. We will leave it at that, for the moment, and return to our models of making friends.

FADING MEMORIES

So far, the rewards of a visit ten years ago and a visit yesterday count the same toward whom you visit tomorrow. But is this plausible? In all kinds of organisms memories fade, and it is a good thing that they do. In a changing world, recent experiences may well be a better guide to the future than those in the distant past. We can build fading memories into our account by keeping only some fraction of the historical weights each time that we update the weights by adding in the payoffs from the day's interactions. If we keep 99 percent of the past weights, memories don't fade very much. If we keep only 10 percent, memories evaporate rapidly like the pheromone trails of ants.

If we build in a moderate rate of memory fade in making friends by keeping 90 percent of the past and run some simulations, a remarkable thing happens. The great variety of visiting probabilities that we described before vanishes, and individual behavior freezes into deterministic visiting patterns. In the situation where only the visitor is reinforced, we find each individual locking on to some other, and visiting that person with probability one. In the situation where both visitor and host are reinforced, the group breaks up into pairs, with each member of a pair always visiting the other member.

If we forget less, for example keeping 99 percent of the past, simulation results begin to look less deterministic and more like those of the original case with perfect memory. But if we remember the moral of our earlier discussion, we may wonder if this is just because we have not waited long enough. Indeed, if we run the simulations for millions of iterations, we can observe the deterministic interaction structure crystallizing out.

It can be demonstrated[10] that any forgetting at all leads to a deterministic structure in the limit. More precisely, in friends I, where only the visitor is reinforced, the limiting states can be *any* deterministic visiting probabilities. In friends II, where there is joint reinforcement, the limiting states may be deterministic pairs or stars. The inclusion of forgetting in the dynamics has converted "phantom stars" into "real stars," which do not disappear in the limit.

Stars can be forced in friends II, by making the number of players odd, so that a partition into pairs is impossible. But in our simulations with ten individuals at 90 percent and 99 percent, stars, although theoretically possible, were not seen. If we forget faster, keeping only 50 percent of the past, we begin to see the structure freezing into states that contain stars.

Stars are, however, fragile arrangements. They are not so fragile as never to be seen. They are fragile in a different sense. Let us introduce mistakes into the model. Suppose that, with some small probability, epsilon, an agent, ignores her past reinforcement and simply picks someone to visit at random.[11] (Of course, this might not be a mistake at all, but rather a form of experimentation.) For fixed rate of forgetting, we let epsilon approach zero and see what limiting states persist with positive probability. These are the *stochastically stable states* that we have met several times before in this book. If there are an even number of players, stars are not stochastically stable. That is the nature of their fragility.

THREE'S COMPANY

In making friends with forgetting, we see a deterministic interaction network crystallizing out of the flux of interaction probabilities. But the networks are very primitive – essentially stopping at the formation of pairs in friends II. Why pairs?

Perhaps the answer is simply because friends II is a two-person interaction. Let us change our story a little. Each morning everyone wakes up, and each chooses two people according to probabilities gotten by her weights. She calls them up, they get together, and they have a party. Everyone gets reinforced – that is, each adds one to her weight for each of the others. We now have a three-person interaction. If we start with six people and run simulations keeping 50 percent of the past, the group regularly breaks up into two cliques of three. Each member of a clique then always chooses that clique's other two members.

This is just a taste of the new phenomena that we may uncover when we move beyond two-person interactions.[12] But we will postpone our discussion of three-person games until we have had the opportunity to consider some nontrivial two-person games.

STAG HUNT

So far, our individuals were all the same, and their interactions were trivial. That helped us concentrate on some basic features of the reinforcement dynamics. Now we can move away from homogeneous populations engaged in trivial interactions and into more interesting territory. Suppose that four of our individuals are stag hunters and six are hare hunters. They meet as before, but now their interaction is the stag hunt game. The game determines the payoffs from their interactions, and the payoffs drive the reinforcement dynamics.

Stag hunters quickly learn to visit only other stag hunters. This is not surprising. Visits to hare hunters are not reinforced, while their visits to stag hunters are. If we wait longer, hare hunters learn to visit only hare hunters. Why does this happen, considering that hare hunters are reinforced equally for visits to anyone? We must remember that reinforcement comes not only from your visits to someone else but also from their visits to you. After stag hunters learn to visit only each other, hare hunters are not visited by stag hunters but they continue to be visited by each other. This tips the balance of reinforcement toward visiting other hare hunters. Eventually the population splits into two mutually exclusive groups, stag hunters and hare hunters, with each group playing a version of friends II among themselves.[13]

The ability of stag hunters to associate exclusively with each other is here delivered by the most modest abilities of reinforcement learning – abilities that might be found across a wide spectrum of organisms. But what a difference these modest abilities can make! Stag hunters prosper. Hare hunters lead a second-rate existence.

REINFORCEMENT AND ROBUSTNESS

Adding a little bit of reinforcement learning for partner choice has dramatically enhanced the prospects for successful stag hunting. Before rushing ahead to explore the territory that has opened up, it is time to ask a few hard questions. How well established is the form of reinforcement learning on which we have focused? And just how robust are these results? Do they really depend on the particular form of reinforcement learning that we have been using, or do they have a more general significance?

In fact, our simple model of positive reinforcement has an interesting pedigree. It is a special case of Duncan Luce's (1959) gamma model of learning. In a famous paper, Richard Herrnstein (1970) used it to give a quantitative version of Thorndike's Law of Effect. Calvin Harley (1981) suggested it as a learning rule that would enable an organism capable of acting in accordance with it to take a shortcut in the evolutionary process – to learn the evolutionarily stable strategy in one generation. Alvin Roth and Ido Erev use it in an interactive context to account for the learning of *strategies* in games.[14] They find that it has quite a bit of success in accounting for a large number of published experimental studies of learning in

games. They suggest two modifications to the basic reinforcement model in order to make it more realistic, and they show
that with these modifications, the learning theory provides an
even better account of the data. We have already considered
the modifications in our discussion of "making friends." They
involve forgetting, where the past is slightly discounted, and an
introduction of errors.

How does forgetting affect the dynamics of choosing partners
in the stag hunt? Stag hunters will still quickly learn to visit only
stag hunters. At that point, the stag hunters are engaged in a
version of friends II with each other. They will lock into pairs,
or occasionally stars.

But with forgetting, it is possible that hare hunters will not
learn to visit only hare hunters. Some may "freeze" into a pattern of visiting a stag hunter. How likely this is depends on the
rate of discounting the past. If we keep very little of the past,
this phenomenon will be observed frequently. If we forget very
little, then for long stretches of time the dynamics will be close
to the dynamics without forgetting, and it will be extremely
improbable for a hare hunter to lock onto a stag hunter. In
simulations with ten agents where, on each update, 90 percent
of the past weights were kept, hare hunters always ended up
visiting hare hunters.

What is a reasonable range of rates of discounting to consider? This will, no doubt, vary from organism to organism and
perhaps from individual to individual. For humans we have
some empirical data. Bereby-Meyer and Erev ran experiments
on simple reinforcement learning with Roth-Erev and other
models of learning in mind. The value of discounting that best
accounts for the data in these experiments keeps .997 of the
past.[15] Other data sets give figures from .900 to .999.[16] With
this range of forgetting, we should expect that hare hunters
will usually pair with hare hunters, just as in the case without
forgetting.

Large error rates will just induce a random component to behavior. But small error or experimentation rates that decline over time will prevent the system from "freezing" into any state and then allow it to settle into a state where both stag hunters and hare hunters meet their own kind.[17]

So far, the prediction of such a state seems reasonably robust. Half of the prediction, that stag hunters learn to meet only stag hunters, should hold for almost any conceivable reinforcement dynamics, because stag hunters get positive reinforcement for meeting a stag hunter but zero reinforcement for meeting a hare hunter. What about that zero? Have we cheated by making this payoff a zero?

Erev and Roth introduce a second model of reinforcement learning with a dynamic aspiration level.[18] Payoffs above the aspiration level are positive, and those below the aspiration level are negative. The aspiration level moves in the direction of the current payoffs – floats up in good times and down in bad times. Total accumulated reinforcement is prevented from becoming zero or negative by the rather crude means of truncation at a very small positive number (such as .0001). Nevertheless, this model fits experimental data remarkably well. Further details of the model are not essential to the point that I want to make.

Suppose that the aspiration levels of stag hunters start at the payoff of a stag hunter against a hare hunter and float upward. Or suppose that they start a bit higher. In either case, they can only speed up the process by which stag hunters find each other, because a stag hunter meeting a hare hunter will then experience negative reinforcement instead of zero reinforcement, while a stag hunter meeting a stag hunter will experience positive reinforcement. The point is really independent of the fine details of the dynamics of negative reinforcement. What is essential is simply that negative reinforcement makes something less likely.

Our general account of choosing partners in the stag hunt game does not seem fragile. General features of reinforcement learning lead stag hunters to meet stag hunters and, at least with high probability, lead hare hunters to meet hare hunters. Once this sort of interaction structure has evolved, the picture that we get from random encounters is inverted. Stag hunters flourish.

DIVISION OF LABOR REVISITED

If choosing partners can make such a crucial difference in the stag hunt, might we not expect it to be of importance in other kinds of interaction? Recall from Part II that the antico-ordination required for a successful division of labor was not easily effected by signals. The difficulty involved what to do when you meet someone who sends the same signal. There is no such difficulty in the present framework. Reinforcement learning quickly leads to a symbiotic pairing in that kind of interaction.

Let us extend the model a little to allow also the option of not specializing at all. There are now three possible strategies. The first is "go it alone" or "jack-of-all-trades." The others are "specialize in A" and "specialize in B." The specialties might be "spearsman" and "beater," or "hunter" and "gatherer." Jack-of-all-trades always gets a payoff of 1. The specialists get a payoff of 2 if they interact with each other, but no payoff at all if they fail to do so.

In a random pairing environment, specialization does not do as well as being a jack-of-all-trades. This is true no matter what the population proportions, provided that all three types are represented. In a large, random-mixing population with half type A specialists and half type B specialists, a small number of jack-of-all-trade players could invade and take over the population.

In a small group of agents who can learn with whom they prefer to associate, the story is quite different. Specialists will then quickly find each other and anticorrelate perfectly. Then, for the same reason that hare hunters end up visiting only hare hunters in the stag hunt game, jack-of-all-trade players will be left associating with each other. Now specialists flourish and the division of labor can become established.

PD VARIATIONS

Hare hunters don't care whom they meet, but in the prisoner's dilemma, everyone wants to meet a cooperator. Shouldn't we then expect that reinforcement learning should always lead both cooperators and defectors to always visit cooperators? Consider a prisoner's dilemma game where the worst payoff, that for cooperating against a defector, is equal to 0. The best payoff, that of defecting against a cooperator is 3, mutual cooperation gets a payoff of 2 for each, and mutual defection gets a payoff of 1. If we run our basic reinforcement dynamics, this is just what we see. Cooperators quickly learn to visit only cooperators, but gradually defectors also learn to visit only cooperators, so that only cooperators are visited in the limit.

Let us change the payoffs so that the premium for defecting against a cooperator is diminished, although the game is still a prisoner's dilemma:

	D	C
D	$2 - e$	$2 + e$
C	0	2

If e were taken to be 0, the game would be neither a prisoner's dilemma nor a stag hunt. If we let $e = 1$, we have the prisoner's dilemma discussed in the last paragraph, which leads to everyone visiting cooperators. When we choose $e = .01$, we have a much attenuated prisoner's dilemma. For this game, simulations of reinforcement learning end up with defectors meeting defectors. Apparently, not all prisoner's dilemmas are created equal.

In rational choice–based game theory, the prisoner's dilemma is the simplest possible game to analyze. Dominance answers all questions, and every game that is qualitatively a prisoner's dilemma generates the same answers. That is no longer the case in the present context. It is true that no matter whether you are a cooperator or a defector, you are reinforced more when you visit a cooperator than when you visit a defector. That is the immediate result of dominance. But remember that your visiting probabilities also depend on reinforcements generated by others' visits to you. That factor was responsible for hare hunters visiting each other in the stag hunt game. Likewise, in prisoner's dilemma, it quickly comes to pass that the only players that visit defectors are other defectors. Thus, for defectors in the prisoner's dilemma, the two factors contributing to reinforcement pull in opposite directions. Relative magnitudes of the payoffs determine the net effect. We have at least two rather different subspecies of prisoner's dilemma.

But both cases that we have discussed share an interesting feature. If we look at total payoffs at the end of the day, cooperators prosper! That is no surprise in the attenuated dilemma where cooperators meet cooperators and defectors meet defectors. But what about the original dilemma where everyone ends up visiting cooperators? Must not defectors do better than cooperators on each of these visits, by the definition of prisoner's dilemma? Indeed they must. But the number of interactions in a day is not the same for each individual. Everyone learns to avoid defectors, and so defectors don't get visited. Their sole payoff is from their visits to others. Cooperators are popular. They get visited by defectors (0 payoff), and by other cooperators (positive payoff). A defector exploits a cooperator for a payoff of 3, and then sits home alone. A cooperator visits another for a payoff of 2 for the visitor and a payoff of 2 for the host. At the end of the day, defectors have an average payoff of 3 and cooperators have an average payoff of 4.

We have identified two types of prisoner's dilemma that behave differently in the context of choosing partners, an attenuated prisoner's dilemma and a "standard" prisoner's dilemma.

	Attenuated PD	Standard PD
Example	$e = .01$	$e = 1$
Pairing	Each visits her own	Everyone visits cooperators
Average payoff	C: 4, D: 3.98	C: 4, D: 3

Other types of prisoner's dilemma are possible in which defectors come out ahead at the end of the day. For instance, we might consider a "strike-it-rich" prisoner's dilemma in which the payoff for defecting against a cooperator is more than twice the payoff of cooperating with a cooperator.[19] Or we could have defecting against a cooperator generate a great enough negative payoff for the cooperator to outweigh the benefit of being visited by other cooperators.

This second possibility raises the question as to why a cooperator should consent to play host to such a visitor. To address this question, we need to modify our model of choosing partners. Each morning everyone wakes up, chooses someone to visit, and calls the person up. The potential host can now (politely or impolitely) decline. She will decline if she judges that the interaction will generate a negative payoff (or one below her aspiration level). How can she judge? If she has had past experience with the potential visitor, she can take the average payoff of past encounters as her estimate; if she has no past experience, she can rely on her initial weight. In this joint-consent model of visiting, defectors will soon have the door slammed in their faces, and will be relegated to visiting other defectors. If we introduce a dynamic aspiration level, the same thing will happen in all prisoner's dilemmas. Cooperators will rapidly learn to visit only cooperators. This will lead to a rise in aspirations, if they were originally low. Then cooperators will refuse to interact with defectors. Defectors, who are reinforced when they visit each other, will then learn to interact only with defectors – completing the process of sorting the population into two mutually exclusive classes, each of which interacts exclusively with itself.

7

COEVOLUTION OF STRUCTURE
AND STRATEGY

IN the previous chapter, we fixed the players' strategies and let the interaction structure evolve, in contrast to most evolutionary game theory, which fixes the interaction structure and lets the strategies evolve. The difference in the two perspectives was apparent. A fluid interaction structure allowed individuals to sort themselves into different groups, often to the benefit of cooperative strategies.

Each perspective might, in some situations, provide an approximately correct view of real behavior. An individual operating in a rigid organization might have to adjust his strategies to fit the prescribed structure. Someone moving to a new town might want to make new friends, but not to change her character. Much of social interaction falls somewhere between the two extremes. Consider the marketplace, where buyers and sellers meet each other, bargain, strike deals, or move on. Or the shifting coalitions in national, corporate, academic, or chimpanzee politics.[1] We need to consider the coevolution of structure and strategy. Agents learn both with whom to interact and what to do. The kind of learning dynamics operative for structure and for strategy may be the same or different. One may be fast and the other slow, or they may proceed at roughly the same rate.

THE STAG HUNT

As in the last chapter, stag hunters and hare hunters begin meeting at random and adjust their interaction probabilities by reinforcement learning. But now, with some probability, a player looks around, and if another strategy is getting a better payoff than his is, he imitates that one. Players' probabilities of imitation are independent. Now, the speed on the reinforcement learning depends on the initial weights. Big initial weights are modified more slowly by reinforcement than are small ones. And the speed of the imitation dynamics depends on the imitation probability. A probability of one would have everything determined by imitation on the first round of play. Small probabilities give us a slow imitation dynamics.

It is easy to see what would happen in extreme cases. If the network structure were fixed, with everyone visiting others with equal probability, and imitation were fast, then hare hunting would have the edge. In a small group, stag hunters might get lucky, blunder into each other, and convert the hare hunters. But more often hare hunters would have the higher average payoff, and the stag hunters would be converted to hare hunting. As the group considered gets larger, it is harder for stag hunters to get lucky, and hare hunters take over more and more. On the other hand, if structure is fluid and strategy revision is slow, stag hunters quickly find each other and prosper. Then slow imitation gradually converts hare hunters to stag hunting.

We can use simulations to get an idea of intermediate behavior between these two extremes. Starting with initial weights of one, we varied the imitation probability with these results:

Imitation Probability	End Result: All Stag	End Result: All Hare
.1	22%	78%
.01	71%	29%

Within this moderate range, the relative speed of structure and strategy revision makes all the difference. Fluid structure, where individuals associate freely, favors the mutually beneficial state where everyone hunts stag.

IMITATION AND BEST-RESPONSE

Imitate-the-best is an interesting strategy-revision dynamics with connections to evolutionary replicator dynamics, but it is not the only interesting way to revise strategies. And in this book we have already seen cases where the choice of strategy-revision dynamics makes a difference in the final outcome. So, with an eye toward what we learned in Chapter 5, let us equip our agents with a little bit of strategic thinking. Now, when an agent revises her strategy, she chooses her best response to the strategy that she has last encountered. If structure is fluid and strategy revision is slow, then, as before, individuals quickly learn to associate with others who have the same strategy. The best response to stag hunting is to hunt stag, and the best response to hare hunting is to hunt hare, and so best-response dynamics just confirms players in what they are doing. The society then consists of two stable social classes, stag hunters and hare hunters. Different strategy-revision dynamics leads to a different social contract.

Both best-response and imitate-the-best have some currency as simplified strategy-revision dynamics. Each stands as the simplest representative of a class of interesting dynamics. Imitate-the-best is related to *imitate with probability proportional to payoff,* which is related to replicator dynamics. Best-response to the last strategy encountered is related to *best-response to some more or less sophisticated inductive estimate of what strategy you are likely to encounter.* People sometimes imitate and sometimes think more strategically. So we might want to consider the case where both strategy-revision dynamics play a role in the process: best-response with probability $p1$; imitate-the-best with probability $p2$.

We now have the relative rates of three adaptive dynamics to consider. For example, suppose we have rapid-interaction structure dynamics, slow best-response and slower imitate-the-best. Stag hunters and hare hunters find their own kind, best-response keeps stag hunters hunting stag and hare hunters hunting hare, and imitate-the-best slowly converts hare hunters to stag hunters, who rapidly learn to associate with other stag hunters. It did not matter that imitate-the-best was slow relative to best-response. What was important was that they were both slow relative to the interaction structure dynamics. We still get the socially beneficial outcome in the long run.

PRISONER'S DILEMMA

The prisoner's dilemma is different. In prisoner's dilemma, by definition, Defect is the best response to any strategy encountered. Best-response dynamics converts cooperators to defectors. Even if everything else is as favorable to cooperation as possible, if best-response is fast relative to imitate-the-best, defectors may be expected to take over the population.

But let us backtrack a little to the case where just two dynamics are operative: reinforcement learning for interaction structure and imitate-the-best for strategy revision. We saw in the last chapter that we must distinguish between different kinds of prisoner's dilemmas. In all prisoner's dilemmas, cooperators learn to visit cooperators. The difference turns on who defectors visit. In attenuated prisoner's dilemmas, the structure dynamics leads defectors to visit defectors. Then, if structure dynamics is fast and imitation dynamics is slow, cooperators do better than defectors on each visit and imitation slowly converts defectors to cooperators, just as it converts hare hunters to stag hunters.

In standard prisoner's dilemmas, defectors learn to visit co-operators. With fast structure-revision dynamics and slow imitation dynamics, we need to see who will be imitated when everyone visits cooperators. To answer this question, we need to be more precise about the meaning of imitate-the-best. If "best" means "best outcome per visit," then imitate-the-best will turn cooperators into defectors. If "best" means "best total outcome at the end of the day," then imitate-the-best will turn defectors into cooperators – because cooperators are visited by other cooperators, and defectors are not. Cooperators are more prosperous than defectors, even though defectors do better on each visit. In standard prisoner's dilemmas, fast structure dynamics and slow imitation dynamics can result in either All Defect or All Cooperate, depending on the kind of imitation.

If we change the story such that the host must consent to the visit, on the basis of a floating aspiration level, cooperators learn not only to visit cooperators but also to slam the door in the face of defectors. Then all prisoner's dilemmas will have an evolution-of-interaction structure like that of attenuated prisoner's dilemmas. Cooperators visit cooperators and defectors visit defectors. Fast structure dynamics and slow imitation dynamics[2] now lead to cooperation.

Now suppose we also add some best-response dynamics. It can't help cooperation, and so in the cases where defection took over without it, defection will take over with it. The question is whether a pinch of best-response will destroy cooperation in those scenarios in which it could otherwise succeed. In the long run – that is, in the limit – this must be true, no matter how slow best-response is relative to the other two dynamics. Even if rapid structure dynamics and slow imitation dynamics has converted everyone to cooperators, an individual will best-respond by changing to defection. Sooner or later – perhaps much later – everyone will best-respond at once. Then everyone will defect. There is no way back.

DIVISION OF LABOR

Let us reconsider the division-of-labor game with the three strategies: jack-of-all-trades, specialist I, and specialist II. Jack-of-all-trades always gets a payoff of 1, no matter whom he meets. He is completely self-reliant, and his meetings involve no more that a tip of the hat. Specialist I and specialist II are better at what they do than Jack-of-all-trades, and when they meet each other, they cooperate for a payoff of 2. But each without the other is as worthless as a termite without the bacteria in its gut that digest cellulose. When specialists don't meet each other, they get a payoff of 0.

We saw in the last chapter that our interaction-structure dynamics leads specialists to visit each other and jacks to visit themselves. In the beginning, when visits are at random, jacks tend to beat specialists. Specialists have only a one-third chance of meeting the appropriate specialist of the other kind. Jacks are assured of their more modest payoff. On average, jacks will do best. But after interaction structure evolves to the point of mutual benefit where one kind of specialist coordinates with the complementary kind, specialists are more fit than jacks.

Suppose we now introduce the possibility of strategy revision. Here, best-response does not raise the difficulties for co-operation that it did in prisoner's dilemma. Best-response to meeting a specialist is to be a complementary specialist, and best-response to meeting a jack is to be a jack. So if structure evolves quickly to the point where specialists coordinate for mutual benefit and jacks visit jacks, best-response just reinforces this structure. The effect of slow best-response dynamics here is benign, just as it was in the stag hunt.

What about strategy revision by imitation? If the interaction structure were frozen at random encounters, then imitate-the-best strategy dynamics would usually convert specialists to jacks, but if structure is fluid and imitation dynamics is slow, imitate-the-best runs the other way. It will slowly convert jacks to specialists, and the newly minted specialists will quickly learn to associate with complementary specialists.

But what is the effect of imitation dynamics on the relative proportions of the different types of specialist? If it is imitate-the-best at the end of the day, then imitation dynamics will tend to balance the numbers of specialist I and specialist II. If there are a lot of specialists II and not many specialists I, then specialists I will get more visits during a day and be more prosperous. Imitation dynamics will tend to convert specialists II to specialists I until their numbers are equal.

Fluid structure and slow imitation and best-response tend to produce a group of equal numbers of complementary specialists, who coordinate perfectly by visiting each other. As in the stag hunt, freedom of association here leads to an optimal state of mutual benefit.

BARGAINING

Each day, each person visits another, they engage in some productive activity, and they bargain over how to divide the good so generated. The activity might just be mutually beneficial trade, with the good generated being the gains generated from trading something you don't need for something you do. Or the good might be more tangible – like the meat of a stag. As before in this book, we consider a simplified version of this game, where the possible strategies are: demand-$\frac{1}{3}$, demand-$\frac{1}{2}$, and demand-$\frac{2}{3}$. Pairs of demands that exceed a total of 100 percent give both parties a payoff of zero, perhaps because they cannot agree on a trade or perhaps because the meat spoils or is stolen because the bargainers can't agree.

If interaction structure evolves according to our reinforcement dynamics, encounters become correlated so that the demands in any encounter total 100 percent. The greedy individuals who demand $\frac{2}{3}$ quickly learn to visit those who demand $\frac{1}{3}$. The extra reinforcement from these visits leads those who demand $\frac{1}{3}$ to visit those who demand $\frac{2}{3}$. Those who demand $\frac{1}{2}$ visit each other.

Once this correlation has been achieved, best-response strategy dynamics simply reinforces players in what they are doing – as in the stag hunt and division of labor. The best response to meeting someone who demands some proportion of the good is to demand the rest. Of the examples that we have considered so far, the toxic effects of best-response have been confined to prisoner's dilemma.

In a curious way, it is imitation dynamics that makes trouble in the context of bargaining. Consider the version of imitation that imitates the strategy with the highest average payoff per encounter. With fast structure dynamics and slow imitation dynamics, compatible types find each other rapidly, and imitation slowly converts others to demand-$\frac{2}{3}$. As long as there are those demand-$\frac{1}{3}$ types in the group, demand-$\frac{2}{3}$ types will find them. Eventually greed will convert all demand-$\frac{1}{3}$ types to demand-$\frac{2}{3}$.

What happens now depends on whether there are any demand-$\frac{1}{2}$ types left in the population, or whether greed has already converted them as well to demanding $\frac{2}{3}$. If there are at least two who demand $\frac{1}{2}$ left who visit each other, then they will each get $\frac{1}{2}$ on each visit and the other types will get nothing. Imitation dynamics will convert all to demanding $\frac{1}{2}$. But if all, or all but one, of those that demand $\frac{1}{2}$ have been converted to demand-$\frac{2}{3}$ at the time when the last of those who demand $\frac{1}{3}$ have been converted, no one will be compatible and all payoffs will be zero.

These unpleasant developments are avoided if imitation works by imitating the strategy that is most prosperous at the end of the day. As some of those who demand $\frac{1}{3}$ get converted, those that remain to make these modest demands get more visits, and the greedy demand-$\frac{2}{3}$ types get fewer visits. Those who are willing to settle for a modest profit get more business. At some point, those who demand $\frac{1}{3}$ would be more prosperous than their greedy counterparts, and this version of imitation dynamics would then tend to convert demand-$\frac{2}{3}$ types back to demand-$\frac{1}{3}$. When we factor in demand-$\frac{1}{2}$ types, it seems that the whole picture may be rather complicated. In bargaining we have the sensitivity to the kind of imitation dynamics that we have already noted in prisoner's dilemma.[3]

STAG HUNT WITH BARGAINING

We have been looking at pieces of a puzzle. Let's put two pieces together.[4] One player visits another and each is either a stag hunter or a hare hunter. If at least one is a hare hunter, then the payoffs are as in the original stag hunt game. Hare hunters are guaranteed hare hunters' payoff. A stag hunter who encounters a hare hunter gets nothing.

But if both are stag hunters, they engage in the hunt but then bargain about how to divide the meat. Their total payoff is now twice the payoff of an individual hunter in the original stag hunt, and they can demand one-third, one-half, or two-thirds of the meat as in the minibargaining game. The original stag hunt game is equivalent to this game, with the players restricted to those who will demand half if they hunt stag.

We now have to consider four types of individual: hare hunter, greedy stag hunter who demands $\frac{2}{3}$, egalitarian stag hunter who demands $\frac{1}{2}$, and modest stag hunter who demands $\frac{1}{3}$. Now the risks associated with stag hunting are multiplied. Not only is there the danger of meeting a hare hunter and getting nothing. For greedy and egalitarian hunters, there is the additional danger of getting nothing when meeting a stag hunter with incompatible demands. That danger does not exist for the modest stag hunter, but his portion of a successful stag hunt may (or may not) be less than that of a hare hunter,

113

depending on the fatness on the hare. If individuals are paired at random, hare hunting is favored.

But if interaction structure is fluid and strategies change only slowly, the familiar story emerges. Suppose that initially all types are equally represented in the population. Stag hunters are only reinforced in encounters with other stag hunters, and so they rapidly learn to visit other stag hunters. Since hare hunters get visited by other hare hunters but not by stag hunters, reinforcement leads hare hunters to visit each other. Furthermore, greedy stag hunters, who demand $\frac{2}{3}$, are only reinforced when they visit modest stag hunters, who demand $\frac{1}{3}$. Greedy stag hunters quickly learn to visit modest ones. Likewise, egalitarian stag hunters learn to avoid greedy ones, and to visit either modest ones or each other. Egalitarians will get more reinforcing visits from other egalitarians than from modest types and will learn to visit each other. Modest types will then learn to visit greedy ones.

Fast structure dynamics sorts the interactions into hare-hare and efficient stag-stag in that stag hunters make bargaining demands that divide the stag without waste or disagreement. Adding strategy-revision dynamics now revisits the considerations that arose in the bargaining game by itself. Best-response dynamics simply reinforces the structure that has been produced by fast structure dynamics. Each player is now making the best response to the strategy with which he or she has learned to associate. Imitation can produce different results, depending on the exact kind of imitation dynamics involved.

A BIGGER STAG HUNT

Real hunts will often involve more than two hunters. How should we think about such stag hunts? Suppose a number of people are hunting a stag and one runs off to chase a hare, as in Rousseau's story. How does this affect the chances of a successful hunt? One possibility would be that one defection ruins the hunt, and this is the way that Rousseau tells the story. The full number are required to surround the stag, and if one defects, the stag escapes through the gap. This is a weakest-link stag hunt; the success of the hunt depends on its weakest link.

Another possibility is that there are too many hunters, and the defection of one doesn't hurt at all (or even helps), although the defection of more would diminish the chances of a successful hunt. Between these extremes there are all sorts of possibilities, which all are generalizations of the two-person stag hunt. They correspond to different ways in which the payoffs to stag hunting may depend on the number of hunters. For example, we might consider a linear three-person stag hunt, where the payoff to a stag hunter is proportional to the number of other stag hunters in the group.

For purposes of comparison, here are examples of a linear three-person stag hunt and a weakest-link three-person stag hunt with the same payoffs for hunting hare and for hunting stag with two other stag hunters:

Linear Three-Person Stag Hunt

	Hare, hare	Hare, stag	Stag, stag
Hunt hare	3	3	3
Hunt stag	0	2	4

Weakest-Link Stag Hunt

	Hare, hare	Hare, stag	Stag, stag
Hunt hare	3	3	3
Hunt stag	0	0	4

Which is more conducive to the development of cooperation, the linear stag hunt or the weakest-link stag hunt? Two
considerations weigh on opposite sides of the matter. On the
face of it, stag hunters get a better deal in linear stag hunt.
They take less of a risk. If they have the bad luck to include a
hare hunter in the group, all is not lost. This contrast would
be amplified if we were to move to a larger stag hunt. But if
interaction structure is fluid, then there is a sense in which the
weakest-link interaction may have an advantage. Stag hunters
may tend to find each other more quickly in the weakest-link
interaction because more is at stake. Stag hunters are never
reinforced for calling up a hare hunter in the weakest-link version, but they are reinforced when they call up a hare hunter
and a stag hunter in the linear version.

If we cast our net a little wider, we encounter a different,
but interesting, three-person game. Remember Hume's row-
boat, which was used in Chapter 1 as an instance of the stag
hunt? If both row, they get to the destination. If one or none
rows, they don't. But the worst thing is to row while the other
doesn't, since you lose the effort of rowing and get nothing for
it. It's a stag hunt. Now suppose that we have three in the boat.
There are only two oars. If everyone is cooperative, two get the
oars and the third sits in the bow and paddles with his hands. He
works as hard as the others, but it really doesn't do any good.
They get to their destination just as fast as if he were a lazy defector and went to sleep. In the weakest-link stag hunt, the best
response to meeting two stag hunters was to join the cooperative effort, but the best response to meeting one of each was to
hunt hare. Here the situation is reversed. If you meet two cooperators, the best payoff goes to the free rider – All Cooperate
is not a Nash equilibrium of this game. But if you meet one of
each, the best response is to grab an oar and row. Our ultimate
interest might be in twenty-one in a boat (twenty can row),

but we might focus on three-in-a boat for simplicity and because it may be a worst-case scenario.[5]

As an example with this qualitative payoff structure, we might consider the following:

Three-in-a-Boat

	Defect, defect	Defect, cooperate	Cooperate, cooperate
Defect	3	3	5
Cooperate	0	4.5	4.5

As a baseline for comparison, we can look at the evolutionary equilibria and evolutionary dynamics in a standard large-population, random-encounter treatment. In both of the stag hunts, hunt hare and hunt stag are both evolutionary stable strategies. Both have an unstable mixed equilibrium, standing between the basins of attraction of these two evolutionarily stable strategies. The magnitude of the basins of attraction varies between the two games. In the linear stag hunt, if more than .75 of the population are stag hunters, then stag hunting will take over the whole population; if less, then hare hunting will go to fixation. The basin of attraction for the state where All Hunt Stag is smaller in the weakest-link stag hunt. Here, the separation between the two basins of attraction falls at about .866. In this setting, as we would expect, cooperation has a bigger hurdle to overcome in the weakest-link game.

In three-in-a-boat, the state of the population where everyone hunts hare (defects) is an evolutionarily stable state, but that in which everyone hunts stag (cooperates) is not. In the latter state, hare hunters who free ride could invade. Although hare hunters do better than stag hunters when almost all of the

117

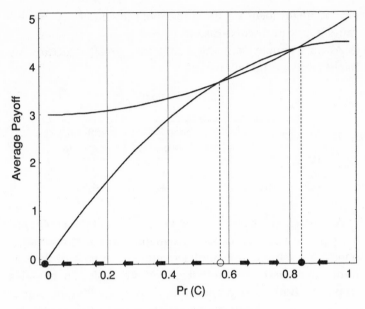

Figure 7.1. Three-in-a-Boat

population hunts hare and also when most of the population hunts stag, they do not always do better, as we can see from Figure 7.1.[6]

There is a second evolutionarily stable state of the population. It is a polymorphism, where most hunt stag but some hunt hare. It has its own basin of attraction, but this is smaller than the basin of attraction of the state where all hunt hare. It is, however, bigger than the basins of attraction of All Hunt Stag in the two stag hunt games. If 56 percent or more of the population hunt stag, the dynamics carries the population to the polymorphic equilibrium where about 83 percent of the population hunt stag. In this setting, prospects for some cooperation seem strongest for three-in-a-boat, and weakest for the weakest-link stag hunt.

118

Unstable Equilibrium That Separates
the Basins of Attraction

Three-in-a-boat	56% Stag
Linear stag hunt	75% Stag
Weakest-link stag hunt	87% Stag

Now let us shift our emphasis 180 degrees. We will fix the strategies of six stag hunters and six hare hunters, and let their interaction probabilities evolve. Each player picks two others with whom to interact, according to his weights, and they play the three-person game. They update their weights for each of the other players by adding the current payoff, just as in the three-friends game of the last chapter. If we assess whether the game is conducive to association of cooperators, we find a ranking that is just the inverse of the previous one. In the weakest-link stag hunt, stag hunters find each other very rapidly. (Typically within a hundred generations, stag hunters will visit other stag hunters with probability 1 to two decimal places.) In the linear stag hunt, stag hunters still find each other, but more slowly. In three-in-a-boat, there is no comparable strong pattern of association that emerges. The forces governing evolution of strategy and evolution of interaction structure are pulling in opposite directions. What will the net effect be?

We start again with six players of each type and allow the coevolution of structure and strategy. Strategy revision is by imitation, with the speed of the process governed by an imitation probability, just as in the two-person case. Our main conclusions regarding the dynamics of the two-person stag hunt continue to hold good for both three-person versions. The outcome is highly dependent on the relative speeds of adaptive dynamics. With frozen random-interaction structure, hare hunting predominates. With fluid interaction structure, stag hunting is favored. When stag hunters find each other, their average payoff at the end of the day goes to three times the

Table 7.1. The Effect of Different Rates of Imitation

	Weakest-Link Stag Hunt		Linear Stag Hunt	
Imitation pr	All Stag	All Hare	All Stag	All Hare
.001	83%	17%	76%	24%
.01	65%	35%	38%	61%
.1	1%	99%	3%	97%

payoff in a three–stag hunter interaction. On average, a stag hunter visits once and is visited twice, and all three interactions are stag-stag-stag interactions. Hare hunters cannot match this payoff, and imitation slowly converts hare hunters to stag hunters.

At intermediate imitation probabilities, the differences between weakest-link and linear three-person stag hunts become evident. In the simulations summarized in Table 7.1, the learning dynamics was run long enough to guarantee that the population went to All Hunt Stag or All Hunt Hare. This took less time (1,000 iterations) for the weakest-link game than for the linear stag hunt (which took up to 10,000 iterations). With rapid imitation at probability .1, the usual outcome in both games is that All Hunt Hare. With very slow imitation at probability .001, stag hunters take over roughly 80 percent of the time in both games. But at an intermediate imitation speed, hare hunters take over more often in the linear stag hunt, but stag hunters have the edge in the weakest-link game. Here, the rapid association that occurs in the weakest-link stag hunt outweighs the payoff advantages to stag hunters in the linear game.

Three-in-a-boat is not really a stag hunt, but rather a three-person hybrid of stag hunt, prisoner's dilemma, and chicken. It poses its own special set of dynamical questions. When we start with six cooperators and six defectors, and let structure and strategy coevolve for a middling amount of time with relatively slow imitation, we see a picture that appears promising for the emergence of some cooperation. Typically, the population moves to a state with seven, eight, or nine cooperators. If, however, we let the process run until the group ends up with All Cooperate or All Defect, it more often than not ends up with All Defect. Slowing down the imitation process improves the numbers a bit, but not much. Why does this happen?

The advantage of free riding when there are many cooperators acts as a barrier that must be surmounted before cooperators can take over. There is no comparable barrier blocking the ascendancy of defectors. In the long run, the population wanders into the zone where defection does better than cooperation, and is carried to a state where All Defect. Free riding is not fatal in the short or medium run, but it appears to be so in the long run.

At this point, the ranking of the three sorts of interaction in terms of how conducive they are for evolution of cooperation has been reversed. In the large population, random-encounter model three-in-a-boat seemed the most favorable environment and weakest link the least favorable. In this small population model, it is the weakest-link interaction that offers the strongest prospects for the evolution of cooperation in the long run.

In the interest of realism, however, there is one further modification of our learning dynamics that needs to be investigated. That involves taking account of "forgetting" or "recency" – the tendency of reinforcement to weight the recent past more heavily than the more distant past. Each morning we will multiply the past weights by a "discount factor." We saw in the last chapter that some empirical estimates of this factor from psychological experiments using Roth-Erev learning models range from .9 to .999.

Taking the discount factor to be .95 and the imitation probability to be .001, ten thousand trials of three-in-a-boat *all* ended up with a population consisting entirely of cooperators. That little bit of discounting the past tended to lock in the interaction structure favorable to cooperators so that they could stay in the seven-eight-nine cooperator area long enough to eventually jump the free-rider barrier. Again, at the other end of our little spectrum, 100 percent of the trials of weakest-link stag hunt ended up with everyone in the population hunting stag. Results with the linear stag hunt were almost as good – 99.9 percent of the trials ended up with All Hunt Stag. These results are robust to small changes in the discount parameter. From a discount of .90 to .99, we see a state of full cooperation emerging almost all the time. In the most empirically realistic version of reinforcement learning, fluid-interaction structure and slow imitation decisively and unambiguously tip the scales in favor of cooperation.

POSTSCRIPT

HOW much progress have we made in addressing the fundamental question of the social contract: "How can you get from the noncooperative hare hunting equilibrium to the cooperative stag hunting equilibrium?" The outlines of a general answer have begun to emerge. Over time there is some low level of experimentation with stag hunting. Eventually a small group of stag hunters comes to interact largely or exclusively with each other. This can come to pass through pure chance and the passage of time in a situation of interaction with neighbors.[1] Or it can happen more rapidly when stag hunters find each other by means of fast interaction dynamics. The small group of stag hunters prospers and can spread by reproduction or imitation. This process is facilitated if reproduction or imitation neighborhoods are larger than interaction neighborhoods. As a local culture of stag hunting spreads, it can even maintain viability in the unfavorable environment of a large, random-mixing population by the device of signaling.

NOTES

PREFACE

1. Hobbes, *Leviathan*, Pt. II, Ch. 17.
2. See Maynard Smith and Szathmary (1995).
3. Hobbes, *Leviathan*, Pt. II, Ch. 17.
4. Aristotle, *Politics*, Bk. I, Ch. 1.
5. See Queller, Ponte, Bozzaro, and Strassman (2003) and Crespi and Springer (2003).

CHAPTER 1. THE STAG HUNT

1. Rousseau, *A Discourse on Inequality*, III.
2. Hume, *A Treatise of Human Nature*, Bk. III, Pt. II, Sec. II, 490.
3. Ibid., Bk. III, Pt. II, Sec. VII, 538.
4. This common-sense generalization is confirmed by carefully controlled game theory experiments. See Van Huyck, Battalio, and Beil (1990).
5. Or the "$\frac{1}{2}$-dominant equilibrium." The two are the same in stag hunt games.
6. Sometimes it is called an assurance game, following Sen (1967).
7. Ed Curley (in his introduction to Hobbes's *Leviathan*), Jean Hampton, Magnus Jiborn, and Peter Vanderschraaf.
8. Hobbes, *Leviathan*, xv, 5, 205.
9. Hume, *Treatise*, 521.
10. This apt phrase is due to Robert Axelrod (1984).
11. If the probability of repetition is low enough, the repeated game is still a prisoner's dilemma. If the probability of repetition is high enough, the stag hunting equilibrium becomes risk dominant.

12. And of Curley's remarks in his introduction to his edition of *Leviathan*, xxviii. The mathematics involved was already known to Newton. The idea that repeated games could explain the viability of cooperation in repeated prisoner's dilemma is already in Luce and Raiffa's 1957 classic *Games and Decisions*.
13. Rawls recommends that agents choose a social contract according to the maximin principle, which would have each agent play it safe by maximizing his or her minimum gain. If agents followed this advice here, they would choose Always Defect.
14. Hume, *Treatise*, Bk. III, Pt. II, Sec. II.
15. See Hofbauer and Sigmund (1988) for an extensive study of the replicator dynamics.
16. Foster and Young (1990).
17. Kandori, Mailath, and Rob (1993).
18. Ibid. and Young (1998).
19. In the risk-dominant equilibrium.
20. That is, when hare hunting is the risk-dominant equilibrium.
21. See Van Huyck, Battalio, and Beil (1990); Clark, Kay, and Sefton (2000); Rankin, Van Huyk, and Battalio (2000); Battalio, Samuelson, and VanHuyck (2001).

PART I. LOCATION

1. Chao and Levin (1981).
2. Durrett and Levin (1994).
3. Pollack (1989); Nowak and May (1992); Nowak, Bonhoeffer, and May (1994); Grim (1995); Hegselmann (1996); Epstein (1998).
4. Hamilton (1964) (1996); Maynard Smith and Szathmary (1995).

CHAPTER 2. BARGAINING WITH NEIGHBORS

1. Nydegger and Owen (1974); Roth, and Malouf (1979); Van Huyck, Battalio, Mathur, Van Huyck, and Ortmann (1995).
2. This is the discrete time version of the replicator dynamics, which is most relevant in comparison to the alternative "bargaining with neighbors" dynamics considered here. There is also a continuous time version. See Hofbauer and Sigmund (1988); Weibull (1995); and Samuelson (1997), as comprehensive references.
3. Bjornerstedt and Weibull (1996); Schlag (1996).

4. Foster and Young (1990); Young (1993a) (1993b).
5. See Ellison (1993) and Axtell, Epstein, and Young (2001) for discussion of expected waiting times.
6. Alexander and Skyrms (1999); Alexander (2000).
7. For example, place a few demand-$\frac{1}{2}$ players in a population of demand-.4 and demand-.6 players with the latter so arranged that there is a demand-.6 type who is the most successful player in the neighborhood of every demand-$\frac{1}{2}$ player.
8. At .9999 level to keep things comparable.
9. For this reason, "frontier advantage" is used to define an unbeatable strategy in Eshel, Sansone, and Shaked (1996).
10. In situating the high strategy of the polymorphic pair in a sea of low-strategy players, we are creating the best-case scenario for the advancement of the polymorphism into the patch of demand-5 players.
11. With some minor complications involving ties.
12. Skyrms (1994) (1996).

CHAPTER 3. STAG HUNT WITH NEIGHBORS

1. My, Willinger, and Ziegelmeyer (forthcoming).
2. A general theory of local interaction with best-response dynamics is developed by Morris (2000). It is not quite correct that local interaction always favors hare hunting. A general theory of local interaction with imitation dynamics is developed by Eshel, Sansone, and Shaked (1996). The former has connections with the part of rational choice theory that studies games of incomplete information. The latter has connections with the part of evolutionary game theory that studies interactions between relatives, using William Hamilton's concept of "inclusive fitness."
3. Pollack (1989); Nowak and May (1992); Grim (1995); Hegselmann (1996); Epstein (1998).
4. See also Eshel, Samuelson, and Shaked (1998).
5. Adapted from an example of Jackson and Watts (2002 a).
6. If the Huntsman were not patient, then the population would spend a smaller proportion of its time hunting stag, but that proportion would still not be negligible, and it would still be true that structure makes a difference. That is the form of the example in Jackson and Watts.
7. Durrett and Levin (1994); Frank (1994); Durrett and Levin (1997).

PART II. SIGNALS

1. See Costerton, Stewart, and Greenberg (1999) and Watnick and Kolter (2000).
2. See Dunlap (2000) and Ruby (2000).
3. This kind of behavior is better known from extensive studies of social amoebae, the cellular slime molds.
4. See Kaiser (1999).
5. See Crespi (2001).

CHAPTER 4. EVOLUTION OF INFERENCE

1. Rousseau, *Discourse*, 94.
2. A more general model of sender-receiver games was introduced and analyzed by Crawford and Sobel (1982).
3. This striking result depends to a certain extent on the modeling decision to make the number of states, messages, and actions equal. Suppose that we add a fourth message to our three-state, three-act game and extend a signaling system equilibrium of the original game by extending the Receiver's strategy to take act 1 if message 4 were received. According to the Sender's strategy, message 4 is never sent, so what the Receiver would do if she received that message is of no consequence. Thus, we do not have a strict equilibrium, and we do not have a Lewis convention of the game with the enlarged message space. This is perhaps not as serious a difficulty as it may at first seem. Let us bracket these concerns for now. We will return to this matter later in a different context.
4. See, for instance, Hauser (1997) and England et al. (1999).
5. This striking conclusion, like Lewis's result that signaling systems are conventions, depends on our modeling assumption that the number of states, messages, and acts are equal. If we add some extra messages to the model, then signaling systems will not be evolutionarily stable strategies in the sense of Maynard Smith and Parker. The reason, as before, is that we can consider a mutant whose strategy specifies a different strategy to a message that is never sent. Such a mutant will not be eliminated. The difficulty, however, does not seem so serious, since the mutant *behaves* just like the native in sending signals and in reacting to signals actually sent. We can shift our attention to classes of behaviorally equivalent strategies

and consider evolutionarily stable classes as ones such that in a population using members of that class, any mutant strategy outside the class will be eliminated. Then the connection between evolutionary stability and signaling systems can be recaptured. The interested reader can find this worked out in Wärneryd (1993).

6. Darwin, *Descent of Man*, 87.
7. Evans et al. (1994).
8. Taylor and Jonker (1978); Schuster and Sigmund (1983).
9. Skyrms (1999).
10. Smith, *Considerations*, 201.
11. See Skyrms (1999).
12. Vervets run out on branches where the leopard cannot follow.
13. Kavanaugh (1980); Cheney and Seyfarth (1990).
14. There are, of course, other ways of giving its meaning, such as terrestrial predator.
15. Nature chooses a random information partition, and the Sender is informed only of the cell that contains the actual situation.

CHAPTER 5. CHEAP TALK

1. Spence(1973) (1974); Zahavi (1975); Zahavi and Zahavi (1997). See also the important clarifications in Grafen (1990).
2. Zahavi and Zahavi (1997).
3. In the experimental literature, however, it is a robust finding that preplay communication increases cooperation in N-person dilemma experiments. See Ledyard (1995), 156–158, for a review. The reasons that this is so are not entirely clear.
4. It is perhaps worth noting that the experimental data are at variance with this conclusion. See Crawford (1998); Charness (2000); Clark, Kay, and Sefton (2000).
5. See Crawford (1998) for a review of earlier literature. Also see Cooper, DeJong, Forsythe, and Ross (1992).
6. Notice that this argument holds good for any assurance game. Nothing depends on the particular payoffs in Aumann's example.
7. This explains why there is no stable equilibrium among the "handshake" strategies <1,stag, hare> and <2,hare,stag>, which cooperate with themselves but not with others. If one were more numerous, it would get a greater payoff, and replicator dynamics would drive it to fixation.

8. See Schlag (1993) and Banerjee and Weibull (2000).
9. See Skyrms (1996).
10. This is from 100,000 trials.
11. These are analyzed in Skyrms (2002).
12. This is from 100,000 trials.
13. For the average information in a signal, we use the Kullback-Leibler discrimination information between the probability measure generated by the population proportions and that generated by conditioning on the signal. The average amount of information in signals in the population is then gotten by averaging over signals. See Kullback and Leibler (1951) and Kullback (1959). This is identical to the amount of information provided by an experiment as defined by Lindley (1956). The "experiment" is looking at your message received, and particular messages correspond to particular experimental results. For more details see Skyrms (2002).
14. The decline does not go to zero for two reasons. One is that the averages include the $1\frac{1}{2}$% of trials that end up in polymorphic equilibria where the signals carry considerable information. The other is that there may be information about response types left even when all demand $\frac{1}{2}$, although that information is only about what would be done if an unsent signal were sent.
15. There are two ways in which one may have a population state that meets the description that I have just given, depending on who does act 1 and who does act 2 when different signals are exchanged. In the simulations, they occur with equal frequency.
16. Large, random pairing.
17. The strategies in these two embedded games are logically independent. Your response if you get one signal entails nothing about response if you get the other.

PART III. ASSOCIATION

1. E. Wilson (1971), Ch.13.
2. Ibid.
3. I have taken some liberties in the statement of these laws. Thorndike's own formulations of them changes over time.
4. This view had the unfortunate consequence of promoting rote learning in schools.

5. For an introduction, see Davis (1999).
6. Othmer and Stevens (1997).

CHAPTER 6. CHOOSING PARTNERS

1. Convergence to two decimal places after a few hundred rounds of visits.
2. That is, a flat probability on the space of possible biases.
3. See de Finetti (1975), 220–221.
4. After 1,000 trials, we see many cases intermediate between symmetry and odd edge out, but after 100,000 trials we only see cases that approximate these.
5. See Skyrms and Pemantle (2000); Pemantle and Skyrms (forthcoming a,b).
6. Pemantle and Skyrms (forthcoming a).
7. See Skyrms and Pemantle (2000), Theorem 3.
8. This is true for many models of negative reinforcement, not just the particular one discussed here.
9. See Fudenberg and Levine (1998); Bereby-Meyer and Erev (1998); Borgers and Sarin (2000).
10. Skyrms and Pemantle (2000).
11. With uniform probability.
12. Time to clique formation is very sensitive to the forgetting rate. For an analysis of three's company, see Pemantle and Skyrms (forthcoming b).
13. See Skyrms and Pemantle (2000), Theorem 6.
14. Roth and Erev (1995); Erev and Roth (1998). They keep the interaction structure constant and let individuals learn how to act, while in this chapter, we keep strategies constant and let individuals learn with whom to interact. In the next chapter we will consider varying both at once.
15. Bereby-Meyer and Erev (1998), 280.
16. Busemeyer and Stout (2002) find normal individuals keeping about 80% of the past, and patients suffering from Huntington's disease keeping about 50%, but they are using different learning models, and so the figures are not directly comparable. They also find out that this rate has considerable variability even among the normal group.

17. In the Roth-Erev model of reinforcement, errors are not applied directly to probabilities, but rather to the current reinforcement. Their effect on probabilities thus declines over time.
18. Dynamic aspiration levels are also discussed in the context of a somewhat different model of reinforcement learning by Borgers and Sarin (2000).
19. Some writers don't even call games like this prisoner's dilemmas, because it would pay "cooperative" players to take turns being the defector against the cooperator. But no matter what you call it, it is a possible kind of interaction that should be considered.

CHAPTER 7. COEVOLUTION OF STRUCTURE AND STRATEGY

1. See de Waal (1998).
2. Either kind of imitation dynamics.
3. The foregoing discussion raises questions about the model. Is it plausible that one modest bargainer can sustain multiple interactions in a day? It depends on the kind of interactions being modeled. A limitation on the number of interactions would be a limit on the value of being popular, and would change the analysis.
4. You could think about putting pieces together in other ways: stag hunt with division of labor, division of labor with bargaining, stag hunt with division of labor, and bargaining.
5. Three-in-a-boat is given its name in Ward (1990). It had previously been discussed as a version of three-person chicken in Taylor and Ward (1982). See also the discussions in Hampton (1987) and in Vanderschraaf (2001).
6. Because this is a three-person game, the payoffs are not linear in population proportions, but rather quadratic.

POSTSCRIPT

1. See Robson and Vega-Redondo (1996), Ely (2002), and Bhaskar and Vega-Redondo (2002) for a demonstration of this general point in models somewhat different from those presented here.

BIBLIOGRAPHY

Alexander, J. M. (2000) "Evolutionary Explanations of Distributive Justice." *Philosophy of Science* 67: 490–516.

Alexander, J. M., and Skyrms, B. (1999) "Bargaining with Neighbors: Is Justice Contagious?" *Journal of Philosophy* 96: 588–598.

Anderlini, L., and Ianni, A. (1996) "Path Dependence and Learning from Neighbors." *Games and Economic Behavior* 13: 141–178.

Anderlini, L., and Ianni, A. (1997) "Learning on a Torus." In *The Dynamics of Norms*. Ed. C. Bicchieri, R. Jeffrey, and B. Skyrms. Cambridge: Cambridge University Press, 87–107.

Aristotle. (2000) *Politics*. Tr. Benjamin Jowett. New York: Dover.

Arthur, W. B., Durlauf, S. N., and Lane, D. A. (1997) *The Economy as an Evolving Complex System II*. Reading, Mass.: Addison Wesley.

Aumann, R. J. (1990) "Nash Equilibria Are Not Self-Enforcing." In *Economic Decision Making, Games, Econometrics and Optimization*. Ed. J. J. Gabzewicz, J.-F. Richard, and L. A. Wolsey. North Holland: Amsterdam, 201–206.

Aumann, R. J., and Myerson, R. (1988) "Endogenous Formation of Links Between Players and Coalitions: An Application of the Shapley Value." In *The Shapley Value*. Ed. A. Roth. Cambridge: Cambridge University Press, 175–191.

Axelrod, R. (1984) *The Evolution of Cooperation*. New York: Basic Books.

Axelrod, R. (1997) *The Complexity of Cooperation: Agent-Based Models of Competition and Collaboration*. Princeton, N.J.: Princeton University Press.

Axelrod, R., and Hamilton, W. D. (1981) "The Evolution of Cooperation." *Science* 211: 1390–1396.

Bibliography

Axtell, R. L., Epstein, J. M., and Young, H. P. (2001) "The Emergence of Classes in a Multi-Agent Bargaining Model." In *Social Dynamics*. Ed. S. Darlauf and H. P. Young. Cambridge, Mass.: MIT Press, 191–211.

Bala, V., and Goyal, S. (1998) "Learning from Neighbors." *Review of Economic Studies* 65: 595–621.

Bala, V., and Goyal, S. (2000) "A Noncooperative Model of Network Formation." *Econometrica* 68: 1181–1231.

Banerjee, A., and Weibull, J. (2000) "Neutrally Stable Outcomes in Cheap-Talk Coordination Games." *Games and Economic Behavior* 32: 1–24.

Battalio, R., Samuelson, L., and Van Huyck, J. (2001) "Optimization Incentives and Coordination Failure in Laboratory Stag Hunt Games." *Econometrica* 61: 989–1018.

Bereby-Meyer, Y., and Erev, I. (1998) "On Learning to Become a Successful Loser: A Comparison of Alternative Abstractions of the Learning Process in the Loss Domain." *Journal of Mathematical Psychology* 42: 266–286.

Bergstrom, T. (2002) "Evolution of Social Behavior: Individual and Group Selection Models." *Journal of Economic Perspectives* 16: 231–238.

Bergstrom, T., and Stark, O. (1993) "How Altruism Can Prevail in an Evolutionary Environment." *American Economic Review* 85: 149–155.

Bhaskar, V. (1998) "Noisy Communication and the Evolution of Cooperation." *Journal of Economic Theory* 82: 110–131.

Bhaskar, V., and Vega-Redondo, F. (forthcoming) "Migration and the Evolution of Conventions." *Journal of Economic Behavior and Organization*.

Binmore, K. (1993) *Playing Fair: Game Theory and the Social Contract I*. Cambridge, Mass.: MIT Press.

Binmore, K. (1998) *Just Playing: Game Theory and the Social Contract II*. Cambridge, Mass.: MIT Press.

Binmore, K., and Samuelson, L. (1997) "Muddling Through: Noisy Equilibrium Selection." *Journal of Economic Theory* 64: 235–265.

Binmore, K., Samuelson, L., and Vaughan, R. (1995) "Musical Chairs: Modeling Noisy Evolution." *Games and Economic Behavior* 11: 1–35.

Bjornerstedt, J., and Weibull, J. (1996) "Nash Equilibrium and Evolution by Imitation." In *The Rational Foundations of Economic Behavior*. Ed. K. Arrow et al. New York: Macmillan, 155–171

134

Bibliography

Blume, L. E. (1993) "The Statistical Mechanics of Strategic Interaction." *Games and Economic Behavior* 4: 387–424.

Blume, L. E. (1995) "The Statistical Mechanics of Best-Response Strategy Revision." *Games and Economic Behavior* 11: 111–145.

Blume, A., DeJong, D. V., Kim, Y.-G., and Sprinkle, G. B. (1998) "Experimental Evidence on the Evolution of Messages in Sender-Receiver Games." *American Economic Review* 88: 1323–1340.

Blume, A., DeJong, D. V., Kim, Y.-G., and Sprinkle, G. B. (2001) "Evolution of Communication with Partial Common Interest." *Games and Economic Behavior* 37: 79–120.

Blume, A., Kim, Y-G., and Sobel, J. (1993) "Evolutionary Stability in Games of Communication." *Games and Economic Behavior* 5: 547–575.

Borgers, T., and Sarin, R. (1997) "Learning Through Reinforcement and the Replicator Dynamics." *Journal of Economic Theory* 77: 1–14.

Borgers, T., and Sarin, R. (2000) "Naive Reinforcement Learning with Endogenous Aspirations." *International Economic Review* 41: 921–950.

Bryant, J. (1994) "Coordination Theory, The Stag Hunt, and Macroeconomics." In *Problems of Coordination in Economic Activity*. Ed. James W. Friedman. Boston: Kluwer, 207–226.

Busemeyer, J. R., and Stout, J. C. (2002) "A Contribution of Cognitive Decision Models to Clinical Assessment: Decomposing Performance on the Bechara Gambling Task." *Psychological Assessment* 14: 253–262.

Bush, R. R., and Mosteller, F. (1951) "A Mathematical Model of Simple Learning." *Psychological Review* 58: 313–323.

Bush, R. R., and Mosteller, F. (1955) *Stochastic Models of Learning*. New York: Wiley.

Catania, A. C. (1999) "Thorndike's Legacy: Learning, Selection and the Law of Effect." *Journal of the Experimental Analysis of Behavior* 72: 425–428.

Chao, L., and Levin, B. (1981) "Structured Habitats and the Evolution of Anticompetitor Toxins in Bacteria." *Proceedings of the National Academy of Sciences of the USA* 78: 6324–6328.

Charness, G. (2000) "Self-Serving Cheap Talk: A Test of Aumann's Conjecture." *Games and Economic Behavior* 33: 177–194.

Cheney, D., and Seyfarth, R. M. (1990) *How Monkeys See the World: Inside the Mind of Another Species*. Chicago: University of Chicago Press.

Bibliography

Chwe, M. (2000) "Communication and Coordination in Social Networks." *Review of Economic Studies* 67: 1–16.

Clark, K., Kay, S., and Sefton, M. (2000) "When Are Nash Equilibria Self-Enforcing? An Experimental Analysis." *International Journal of Game Theory* 29: 495–515.

Cooper, R., DeJong, D., Forsythe, R., and Ross, T. W. (1992) "Communication in Coordination Games." *Quarterly Journal of Economics* 107: 739–771.

Costerton, J. W., Stewart, P. S., and Greenberg, E. P. (1999) "Bacterial Biofilms: A Common Cause of Persistent Infections." *Science* 284: 1318–1322.

Crawford, V. (1998) "A Survey on Experiments on Communication via Cheap Talk." *Journal of Economic Theory* 78: 286–298.

Crawford, V., and Sobel, J. (1982) "Strategic Information Transmission." *Econometrica* 50: 1431–1451.

Crespi, B. J. (2001) "The Evolution of Social Behavior in Microorganisms." *Trends in Ecology and Evolution* 16: 178–183.

Crespi, B., and Springer, S. (2003) "Social Slime Molds Meet Their Match." *Science* 299: 56–57.

Danielson, P. (1992) *Artificial Morality*. London: Routledge.

Danielson, P. (2002) "Competition Among Cooperators: Altruism and Reciprocity." *Proceedings of the National Academy of Sciences* 99 (supplement 3): 7237–7242.

Darwin, C. (1882) *The Descent of Man and Selection in Relation to Sex*. 2d. ed. New York: D. Appleton.

Davis, B. (1990) "Reinforced Random Walk." *Probability Theory and Related Fields* 84: 203–229.

Davis, B. (1999) "Reinforced and Perturbed Random Walks." In *Random Walks* (Bolyai Society of Mathematical Studies 9). Ed. Pál Révést and Bálint Tóth. Budapest: János Bolyai Mathematical Society, 113–126.

De Finetti. B. (1975) *Theory of Probability*. Vol. 2. Trans. A. Machi and A. Smith. New York: John Wiley.

De Waal, Frans. (1998) *Chimpanzee Politics: Sex and Power Among the Apes*. 2d. ed. Baltimore: Johns Hopkins University Press.

Diaconis. P. (1988) "Recent Progress in DeFinetti's Notion of Exchangeability." In *Bayesian Statistics*. Ed J. Bernardo, M. DeGroot, D. Lindley, and A. Smith. New York: Oxford University Press, 111–125.

Dieckmann, T. (1999) "The Evolution of Conventions with Mobile Players." *Journal of Economic Behavior and Organization* 38: 93–111.

Dunlap, P. V. (2000) "Quorum Regulation of Luminescence in *Vibrio Fischeri*." In *Molecular Marine Biology*. Ed. D. H. Bartlett. Norfolk, U.K.: Horizon Scientific Press, 3–21.

Durlauf, S. (1996) "A Theory of Persistant Income Inequality." *Journal of Economic Growth* 1: 75–93.

Durlauf, S., and Young, H. P., eds. (2001) *Social Dynamics*. Cambridge, Mass.: MIT Press.

Durrett, R., and Levin, S. (1994) "The Importance of Being Discrete (and Spatial)." *Theoretical Population Biology* 46: 363–394.

Durrett, R., and Levin, S. (1997) "Allelopathy in Spatially Distributed Populations." *Journal of Theoretical Biology* 185: 165–171.

Ellison, G. (1993) "Learning, Local Interaction and Coordination." *Econometrica* 61: 1047–1071.

Ellison, G. (2000) "Basins of Attraction, Long-Run Stochastic Stability and the Speed of Step-by-Step Evolution." *Review of Economic Studies* 67: 17–45.

Ely, J. (2002) "Local Conventions." *Advances in Theoretical Economics*. Vol. 2, n. 1, Article 1. http://www.bepress.com/bejte/advances/vol2/iss1/art1.

England, R. R., Hobbs, G., Bainton, N. J., and Roberts, D. McL. (1999) *Microbial Signalling and Communication*. Cambridge: Cambridge University Press.

Epstein, J. M. (1998) "Zones of Cooperation in Demographic Prisoner's Dilemma." *Complexity* 4: 36–48.

Epstein, J., and Axtell, R. (1996) *Growing Artificial Societies: Social Science from the Bottom Up*. Cambridge, Mass.: MIT Press.

Erev, I., Bereby-Meyer, Y., and Roth, A. (1999) "The Effect of Adding a Constant to All Payoffs: Experimental Investigation and Implications for Reinforcement Learning." *Journal of Economic Behavior and Organization* 39: 111–128.

Erev, I., and Roth, A. E. (1998) "Predicting How People Play Games: Reinforcement Learning in Experimental Games with Unique Mixed Strategy Equilibria." *American Economic Review* 88: 848–881.

Eshel, I., Samuelson, L., and Shaked, A. (1998) "Altruists, Egoists and Hooligans in a Local Interaction Model." *American Economic Review* 88: 157–179.

Eshel, I., Sansone, E., and Shaked, A. (1996) "Evolutionary Dynamics of Populations with a Local Interaction Structure." ELSE Working

Papers n. 25, ESRC Centre on Economics Learning and Social Evolution, University College, London.

Estes, W. K. (1950) "Toward a Statistical Theory of Learning." *Psychological Review* 57: 94–107.

Evans, C. S., Evans, C. L., and Marler, P. (1994) "On the Meaning of Alarm Calls: Functional Reference in an Avian Vocal System." *Animal Behavior* 73: 23–38.

Farrell, J., and Rabin, M. (1996) "Cheap Talk." *Journal of Economic Perspectives* 10: 103–118.

Foster, D. P., and Young, H. P. (1990) "Stochastic Evolutionary Game Dynamics." *Theoretical Population Biology* 28: 219–232.

Frank, S. (1994) "Spatial Polymorphism of Bacteriocins and other Allelopathic Traits." *Evolutionary Ecology* 8: 369–386.

Fudenberg, D., and Levine, D. K. (1998) *A Theory of Learning in Games.* Cambridge, Mass.: MIT Press.

Goyal, S., and Vega-Redondo, F. (2001) "Network Formation and Social Coordination." Working Paper WP 481, Queen Mary College, University of London, Department of Economics.

Grafen, A. (1990) "Biological Signals as Handicaps." *Journal of Theoretical Biology* 144: 517–546.

Grim, P. (1995) "The Greater Generosity of the Spatialized Prisoner's Dilemma." *Journal of Theoretical Biology* 173: 353–359.

Grim, P., Mar, G., and St. Denis, P. (1998) *The Philosophical Computer: Exploratory Essays in Philosophical Computer Modeling.* Cambridge, Mass.: MIT Press.

Hamilton, W. (1964) "The Genetical Evolution of Social Behavior I and II." *Journal of Theoretical Biology* 7: 1–52.

Hamilton, W. (1996) *Narrow Roads of Geneland.* San Francisco: W. H. Freeman.

Hampton, J. (1987) "Free-Rider Problems in the Production of Collective Goods." *Economics and Philosophy* 3: 245–273.

Hampton, J. (1997) *Hobbes and the Social Contract Tradition.* New York: Cambridge University Press.

Harley, C. B. (1981) "Learning the Evolutionarily Stable Strategy." *Journal of Theoretical Biology* 89: 611–633.

Harms, W. (1999) "Biological Altruism in Hostile Environments" *Complexity* 5: 23–28.

Harms, W. (2001) "Cooperative Boundary Populations: The Evolution of Cooperation on Mortality Risk Gradients." *Journal of Theoretical Biology* 213: 299–313.

Harsanyi, J., and Selten, R. (1988) *A General Theory of Equilibrium Selection in Games*. Cambridge Mass.: MIT Press.

Hauser, M. D. (1997) *The Evolution of Communication*. Cambridge, Mass.: MIT Press.

Hegselmann, R. (1996) "Social Dilemmas in Lineland and Flatland." In *Frontiers in Social Dilemmas Research*. Ed. W. Liebrand and D. Messick. Berlin: Springer, 337–362.

Herrnstein, R. J. (1970) "On the Law of Effect." *Journal of the Experimental Analysis of Behavior* 13: 243–266.

Hobbes, T. (1668) *Leviathan*. Ed. and trans. E. Curley (1994). Indianapolis: Hackett.

Hofbauer, J., and Sigmund, K. (1988) *The Theory of Evolution and Dynamical Systems*. Cambridge: Cambridge University Press.

Huberman, B., and Glance, N. (1993) "Evolutionary Games and Computer Simulations." *Proceedings of the National Academy of Sciences of the USA* 90: 7716–7718.

Hume, D. (1739) *A Treatise of Human Nature*. Ed. L. A. Selby-Bigge (1949). Oxford: Clarendon.

Ioannides, Y. M. (1997) "Evolution of Trading Structures." In *The Economy as an Evolving Complex System II*. Ed. W. B. Arthur, S. N. Durlauf, and D. A. Lane. Reading, Mass.: Addison Wesley.

Iwasa, Y., Nakamura, M., and Levin, S. (1998) "Allelopathy of Bacteria in a Lattice Population: Competition Between Colicin-Sensitive and Colicin-Producing Strains." *Evolutionary Ecology* 12: 785–802.

Jackson, M., and Watts, A. (2002 a) "On the Formation of Interaction Networks in Social Coordination Games" *Games and Economic Behavior* 41: 265–291.

Jackson, M., and Watts, A. (2002 b) "The Evolution of Social and Economic Networks." *Journal of Economic Theory* 106: 265–295.

Jervis, R. (1978) "Cooperation Under the Security Dilemma." *World Politics* 30: 167–214.

Jiborn, M. (1999) *Voluntary Coercion*. Lund: Lund University.

Kahneman, D., and Tversky, A. (1979) "Prospect Theory: An Analysis of Decision Under Risk." *Econometrica* 47: 263–291.

Kaiser, D. (1999) "Intercellular Signaling for Multicellular Morphogenesis." In *Microbial Signalling and Communication*. Ed. R. R. England et al. Cambridge: Cambridge University Press, 140–160.

Kalai, E., and Smordinski, M. (1975) "Other Solutions to Nash's Bargaining Problem." *Econometrica* 43: 513–518.

Bibliography

Kandori, M., Mailath, G., and Rob, R. (1993) "Learning, Mutation and Long-Run Equilibria in Games." *Econometrica* 61: 29–56.

Kavanaugh, M. (1980) "Invasion of the Forest by an African Savannah Monkey: Behavioral Adaptations." *Behavior* 73: 238–260.

Kim, Y-G., and Sobel, J. (1995) "An Evolutionary Approach to Preplay Communication." *Econometrica* 63: 1181–1193.

Kirman, A. (1997) "The Economy as an Evolving Network." *Journal of Evolutionary Economics* 7: 339–353.

Kitcher, P. (1993) "The Evolution of Human Altruism." *Journal of Philosophy* 90: 497–516.

Kohler, T. A., and Gumerman, G. J. (2000) *Dynamics in Human and Primate Societies*. New York: Oxford University Press.

Kropotkin, P. (1908) *Mutual Aid: A Factor in Evolution*. London: Heinemann. The chapters were originally published in *Nineteenth Century*: September and November 1890, April 1891, January 1892, August and September 1894, and January and June 1896.

Kullback, S. (1959) *Information Theory and Statistics*. Wiley: New York.

Kullback, S., and Leibler, R. A. (1951) "On Information and Sufficiency." *Annals of Mathematical Statistics* 22: 79–86.

Ledyard, J. O. (1995) "Public Goods: A Survey of Experimental Research." In *The Handbook of Experimental Economics*. Ed. J. Kagel and A. Roth. Princeton, N.J.: Princeton University Press, 111–194.

Lewis, D. K. (1969) *Convention: A Philosophical Study*. Oxford: Blackwell.

Lindgren, K., and Nordahl, M. (1994) "Evolutionary Dynamics in Spatial Games." *Physica D* 75: 292–309.

Lindley, D. (1956) "On a Measure of the Information Provided by an Experiment." *Annals of Mathematical Statistics* 27: 986–1005.

Luce, R. D. (1959) *Individual Choice Behavior*. New York: Wiley.

Luce, R. D. (2000) *Utility of Gains and Losses: Measurement-Theoretical and Experimental Approaches*. Mahwah, N.J.: Erlbaum.

Luce, R. D., and Raiffa, H. (1957) *Games and Decisions*. New York: Wiley.

Macy, M. (1991) "Learning to Cooperate: Stochastic and Tacit Collusion in Social Exchange." *American Journal of Sociology* 97: 808–843.

Macy, M., and Flache, A. (2002) "Learning Dynamics in Social Dilemmas." *Proceedings of the National Academy of Sciences* 99 (supplement 3): 7229–7236.

Macy, M., and Sato, Y. (2002) "Trust, Cooperation and Market Formation in the U.S. and Japan." *Proceedings of the National Academy of Sciences* 99 (supplement 3): 7214–7220.

Bibliography

Mailath, G. J., Samuelson, L., and Shaked, A. (1997) "Correlated Equilibrium and Local Interactions." *Economic Theory* 9: 551–556.

Maynard Smith, J. (1964). "Group Selection and Kin Selection." *Nature* 201: 1145–1146.

Maynard Smith, J., and Parker, G. (1976) "The Logic of Asymmetric Contests." *Animal Behavior* 24: 159–179.

Maynard Smith, J., and Price, G. (1973) "The Logic of Animal Conflicts." *Nature* 246: 15–18.

Maynard Smith, J., and Szathmary, E. (1995) *The Major Transitions in Evolution*. New York: W. H. Freeman.

Morris, S. (2000) "Contagion." *Review of Economic Studies* 67: 57–78.

My, K. B., Willinger, M., and Ziegelmeyer, A. (forthcoming) "Global Versus Local Interaction In Coordination Games: An Experimental Investigation" *Journal of Evolutionary Economics*.

Nash, J. (1950) "The Bargaining Problem." *Econometrica* 18: 155–162.

Nowak, M. A., Bonhoeffer, S., and May, R. M. (1994) "Spatial Games and the Maintenance of Cooperation." *Proceedings of the National Academy of Sciences of the USA* 91: 4877–4881.

Nowak, M. A., and May, R. M. (1992) "Evolutionary Games and Spatial Chaos." *Nature* 359: 826–829.

Nydegger, R. V., and Owen, G. (1974) "Two-Person Bargaining: An Experimental Test of the Nash Axioms." *International Journal of Game Theory* 3: 239–250.

Oechssler, J. (1997) "Decentralization and the Coordination Problem." *Journal of Economic Behavior and Organization* 32: 119–135.

Othmer, H. G., and Stevens, A. (1997) "Aggregation, Blowup and Collapse: The ABC's of Taxis in Reinforced Random Walks." *SIAM Journal of Applied Mathematics* 57: 1044–1081.

Pemantle, R. (1990) "Nonconvergence to Unstable Points in Urn Models and Stochastic Approximations." *Annals of Probability* 18: 698–712.

Pemantle, R., and Skyrms, B. (forthcoming a) "Reinforcement Schemes May Take a Long Time to Exhibit Limiting Behavior."

Pemantle, R., and Skyrms, B. (forthcoming b) "Network Formation by Reinforcement Learning: The Long and the Medium Run."

Pemantle, R., and Skyrms, B. (forthcoming c) "Time to Absorption in Discounted Reinforcement Models." *Stochastic Processes and Their Applications*.

Pollack, G. B. (1989) "Evolutionary Stability on a Viscous Lattice." *Social Networks* 11: 175–212.

Bibliography

Queller, D., Ponte, E., Bozzaro, S., and Strassman, J. (2003) "Single-Gene Greenbeard Effects in the Social Amoeba *Dictyostelium discoideum*." *Science* 299: 105–106.

Rankin, F. W., Van Huyck, J. B., and Battalio, R. (2000) "Strategic Similarity and Emergent Conventions: Evidence from Similar Stag Hunt Games." *Games and Economic Behavior* 32: 315–337.

Robson, A. J. (1990) "Efficiency in Evolutionary Games: Darwin, Nash and the Secret Handshake." *Journal of Theoretical Biology* 144: 379–396.

Robson, A. J., and Vega-Redondo, F. (1996) "Efficient Equilibrium Selection in Evolutionary Games with Random Matching." *Journal of Economic Theory* 70: 65–92.

Roth, A. E., and Erev, I. (1995) "Learning in Extensive Form Games: Experimental Data and Simple Dynamic Models in the Intermediate Term." *Games and Economics Behavior* 8: 164–212.

Roth, A, E., and Malouf, M. (1979) "Game Theoretic Models and the Role of Information in Bargaining." *Psychological Review* 86: 574–594.

Rousseau, J. (1984) *A Discourse on Inequality*. Trans. M. Cranston. New York: Penguin Books.

Ruby, E. G. (2000) "The *Euprymna scolopes-Vibrio fischeri* Symbiosis: A Biomedical Model for the Study of Bacterial Colonization of Animal Tissue." In *Molecular Marine Biology*. Ed. Douglas H. Bartlett. Norfolk, U.K.: Horizon Scientific Press.

Samuelson, L. (1997) *Evolutionary Games and Equilibrium Selection*. Cambridge, Mass.: MIT Press.

Schelling, T. (1960) *The Strategy of Conflict*. Cambridge, Mass.: Harvard University Press.

Schelling, T. (1971) "Dynamics Models of Segregation." *Journal of Mathematical Sociology* 1: 143–186.

Schelling, T. (1978) *Micromotives and Macrobehavior*. New York: Norton.

Schlag, K. "Cheap Talk and Evolutionary Dynamics." Working Paper, Bonn University, Department of Economics.

Schlag, K. "When Does Evolution Lead to Efficiency in Communication Games?" Working Paper, Bonn University, Department of Economics.

Schlag, K. (1996) "Why Imitate, and If So How? A Boundedly Rational Approach to Multi-Armed Bandits." *Journal of Economic Theory* 78: 130–156.

Schuster, P., and Sigmund, K. (1983) "Replicator Dynamics." *Journal of Theoretical Biology* 100: 535–538.

Sen, A. (1967) "Isolation, Assurance, and the Social Rate of Discount." *Quarterly Journal of Economics* 81: 112–124.

Shimkets, L. J. (1999) "Intercellular Signaling During Fruiting-Body Development of *Myxococcus xanthus*." *American Review of Microbiology* 53: 525–49.

Sigmund, K. (1993) *Games of Life*. Oxford: Oxford University Press.

Skyrms, B. (1994) "Sex and Justice." *Journal of Philosophy* 91: 305–20.

Skyrms, B. (1996) *Evolution of the Social Contract*. New York: Cambridge University Press.

Skyrms, B. (1998) "The Shadow of the Future." In *Rational Commitment and Social Justice: Essays for Gregory Kavka*. Ed. J. Coleman and C. Morris. Cambridge: Cambridge University Press, 12–22.

Skyrms, B. (1999) "Stability and Explanatory Significance of Some Simple Evolutionary Models." *Philosophy of Science* 67: 94–113.

Skyrms, B. (2000) "Evolution of Inference." In *Dynamics of Human and Primate Societies*. Ed. T. Kohler and G. Gumerman. New York: Oxford University Press, 77–88.

Skyrms, B. (2001) "The Stag Hunt." Presidential Address of the Pacific Division of the American Philosophical Association. In *Proceedings and Addresses of the APA* 75: 31–41.

Skyrms, B. (2002) "Signals, Evolution and the Explanatory Power of Transient Information." *Philosophy of Science* 69: 407–428.

Skyrms, B., and Pemantle, R. (2000) "A Dynamic Model of Social Network Formation." *Proceedings of the National Academy of Sciences of the USA* 97: 9340–9346.

Skyrms, B., and Vanderschraaf, P. (1997) "Game Theory." In *The Handbook of Practical Logic*. Ed. Philippe Smets. Dordrecht: Kluwer.

Slikker, M., and van den Nouweland, A. (2000) "Network Formation with Costs of Establishing Links." *Review of Economic Design* 5: 333–362.

Smith, A. (1761) "Considerations Concerning the First Formation of Languages." Reprinted in *Lectures on Rhetoric and Belles Lettres*. Ed. J. C. Bryce (1983). Oxford: Oxford University Press, 201–226.

Sobel, J. (1993) "Evolutionary Stability and Efficiency." *Economic Letters* 42: 301–312.

Sober, E., and Wilson, D. S. (1998) *Unto Others: The Evolution and Psychology of Unselfish Behavior*. Cambridge, Mass.: Harvard University Press.

Bibliography

Spence, A. M. (1973) "Job Market Signaling." *Quarterly Journal of Economics* 87: 355–374.

Spence, A. M. (1974) *Market Signaling: Informational Transfer in Hiring and Related Processes.* Cambridge, Mass.: Harvard University Press.

Sugden, R. (1986) *The Economics of Co-operation, Rights, and Welfare.* New York: Blackwell.

Suppes, P., and Atkinson, R. C. (1960) *Markov Learning Models for Multiperson Interactions.* Stanford, Calif.: Stanford University Press.

Taylor, M., and Ward, H. (1982) "Chickens, Whales and Lumpy Goods: Alternative Models of Public Goods Provision." *Political Science* 30: 350–370.

Taylor, P., and Jonker, L. (1978) "Evolutionarily Stable Strategies and Game Dynamics." *Mathematical Biosciences* 40: 145–156.

Tesfatsion, L. (2002) "Economic Agents and Markets as Emergent Phenomena." *Proceedings of the National Academy of Sciences* 99 (supplement 3): 7191–7192.

Thorndike, E. L. (1907) *The Elements of Psychology.* 2d. ed. New York: A. G. Seiler.

Vanderschraaf, P. (1998) "The Informal Game Theory in Hume's Account of Convention." *Economics and Philosophy* 14: 251–257.

Vanderschraaf, P. (2001) *Learning and Coordination: Inductive Deliberation, Equilibrium and Convention.* London: Routledge.

Van Huyck, J. B., Battalio, R. C., and Beil, R. O. (1990) "Tacit Coordination Games, Strategic Uncertainty and Coordination Failure." *American Economic Review* 80: 234–248.

Van Huyck, J., Batallio, R., Mathur, S., Van Huyck, P., and Ortmann, A. (1995) "On the Origin of Convention: Evidence from Symmetric Bargaining Games." *International Journal of Game Theory* 34: 187–212.

Ward, H. (1990) "Three Men in a Boat, Two Must Row: An Analysis of a Three-Person Chicken Pregame." *Journal of Conflict Resolution* 34: 371–400.

Wärneryd, K. (1991) "Evolutionary Stability in Unanimity Games with Cheap Talk." *Economic Letters* 39: 295–300.

Wärneryd, K. (1993) "Cheap Talk, Coordination and Evolutionary Stability." *Games and Economic Behavior* 5: 532–546.

Watnick, P., and Kolter, R. (2000) "Biofilm, City of Microbes." *Journal of Bacteriology* 182: 2675–2679.

Watts, A. (2001) "A Dynamic Model of Network Formation" *Games and Economic Behavior* 34: 331–341.

Bibliography

Weibull, J. (1995) *Evolutionary Game Theory*. Cambridge, Mass.: MIT Press.

Weisbuch, G., Kirman, A., and Herreiner, D. (2000) "Market Organization and Trading Relationships." *Economic Journal* 110: 411–436.

Williams, G. C. (1966) *Adaptation and Natural Selection: A Critique of Some Current Evolutionary Thought*. Princeton, N.J.: Princeton University Press.

Wilson, D. S. (1975) "A Theory of Group Selection." *Proceedings of the National Academy of Sciences of the USA* 72: 143–146.

Wilson, E. O. (1971) *The Insect Societies*. Cambridge, Mass.: Harvard University Press.

Wright, S. (1943) "Isolation by Distance." *Genetics* 28: 114–138.

Wynne-Edwards, V. C. (1962) *Animal Dispersion in Relation to Social Behavior*. London: Oliver and Boyd.

Yaari, M., and Bar-Hillel, M. (1981) "On Dividing Justly." *Social Choice and Welfare* 1: 1–24.

Young, H. P. (1993a) "The Evolution of Conventions." *Econometrica* 61: 57–84.

Young, H. P. (1993b) "An Evolutionary Model of Bargaining." *Journal of Economic Theory* 59: 145–168.

Young, H. P. (1998) *Individual Strategy and Social Structure*. Princeton, N.J.: Princeton University Press.

Young, H. P. (May 1999) "Diffusion in Social Networks." Working Paper No. 2, Center on Social and Economic Dynamics, Brookings Institution.

Zahavi, A. (1975) "Mate selection – a Selection for a Handicap." *Journal of Theoretical Biology* 53: 205–214.

Zahavi, A., and Zahavi, A. (1997) *The Handicap Principle*. Oxford: Oxford University Press.

INDEX